Homeschooling *Discipleship*
Much More Than ABC's and 123's

Kimberly Williams

Copyright © 2013 Kimberly Williams

All rights reserved. No part of this book may be reproduced in any form without the expressed permission of the author.

All Scripture references used in this book are from the King James Version.

ISBN:0615847641
ISBN-13: 978-0615847641

Printed in the United States of America

What People Are Saying

"In a church so focused on worldwide missions, we often neglect the obligation of making disciples in our own home. This book takes the command 'Go ye therefore and teach all nations....' right to your own living room." Brian & Jayna Harvison, homeschooling parents

"I've known Kimberly Williams as a friend and author for several years. Her heart for Christian families and discipling the next generation in the ways of God is unmistakable. In this book, Kimberly shares timeless wisdom that will expand your vision for homeschooling and help you see it as so much more than reading, writing, and arithmetic. I've said it myself many times: Homeschooling is about raising the next generation for the glory of God. This book will help you do just that." – Jonathan Lewis, Editor, Home School Enrichment Magazine

"Kimberly hits the nail on the head: the relationship of home discipleship must start in the heart of the parents. When mom nourishes her own spiritual life and deepens her own relationship with God, she then has the resources with which to encourage her own children. "Home Discipleship" is about spiritual growth; Lord, may it begin with me!" – Lea Ann Garfias, Director of Web Publishing, Home Educating Family

Contents

	Introduction	1
1	The Biblical Mandate	5
2	The Structure of the Home	15
3	The Proper Perspective	25
4	The Higher Education	33
5	The Fundamentals	42
6	The Standards & Goals	50
7	The Practicalities	63
8	The Individuality	73
9	The Opposition	82
10	The Results	91
11	The Distinction	98
12	The Conclusion	108
	Favorite Resources	116
	About the Author	118

Dedication

To my Lord and Savior, who is my all in all. It is He that brought me from darkness to light, gave me my husband and three beautiful blessings, placed us on the path of home education, and has been molding and shaping our family all these years. Lord, without You life would be meaningless.

To my husband who is my greatest encourager and best friend. He lovingly leads and guides his family in the nurture and admonition of the Lord. Love, you make being a wife and mother a pure delight.

To my precious, sweet children who bring joy and laughter to our home. Aaron, Abigail, and Andrew, you are all a gift from God and I thank the Lord for each of you.

To all who read this book, with a heart's desire to disciple their children in the ways of the Lord. May God bless your family as you strive to follow Him.

Introduction

A generation ago, the homeschooling movement was considered to be at best cutting-edge, eccentric, and alternative. At its worst it was considered strange, rare, and in some states illegal. But today the movement has become more main-stream. Currently with over two million home educated children in the United States, homeschooling may be the fastest growing form of education in our country.

There are many reasons parents take on the responsibility to educate their children at home. The rationale varies, but often at the top of the list are religious or moral reasons. With the tearing down of Christian values in our society, it is understandable why parents want to bring their children back home. Christians are waking up to the fact that education is not amoral. The education that children receive shapes their lives in all forms. Some parents are academically motivated. They want to give their children a better education than the public system can offer. Studies are proving that this is a very valid reason. For example, in his 2011 research Dr. Brian D. Ray, at the National Home Education Research Institute (*www.nheri.org*), concluded that home-educated students typically score 15 to 30 percentile points above public-school students on standardized academic achievement tests. Other parents say that health reasons or special needs of their children are the main motivation for home education. Social or political reasons, as well as family problems or safety concerns, are sometimes voiced. Often the reasons are a combination of several factors and are as many and diverse as our nation and the people in it.

As homeschooling continues to grow, more and more will give it a try due to it being the "newest fad". Homeschooling is more familiar than it used to be. People are talking about it. Homeschoolers like the Duggar family, from TLC's show 19 Kids and Counting, have made homeschooling a well-known topic. Athletes like Tim Tebow have been influential in bringing homeschooling to the public eye. Hollywood stars who homeschool their children are setting the example and include well known celebrities like Kirk Cameron and Lisa Whelchel.

Book stores are lined with books on the ins and outs of the homeschooling movement. They include everything from:

- Why should we homeschool?
- How do we homeschool?
- How do we stay motivated in the process?

So, you might ask, why do we need another book on homeschooling? While this book is geared toward homeschooling families, it is not a book specifically about homeschooling. The term "homeschooling" was not chosen because "school" by definition is an institution for teaching children. The Christian home is so much more. This is also not a book on education. By definition "education" is the knowledge and development resulting from an educational process. While knowledge is good, without wisdom from God to apply knowledge it becomes futile. The principle behind this book and the foundation that we will build upon is discipleship within the home. It is much more than ABC's and 123's.

Home Discipleship is written exclusively for Christian parents who understand and accept the Word of God as the final authority on all things, including those that relate to the family, home, and education of their children. It is written for those who truly believe that the Bible is our all sufficient rule of faith and practice. It is written for parents who want more for their children than what the world offers. And it is written for those who feel a higher calling in the education of their children, a calling that goes above and beyond the educational standards of today's society. My prayer is that Christian families will benefit and be encouraged as we delve deep into the discipleship of our children and that through Home Discipleship we will shape the future generation one family at a time.

Chapter 1
The Biblical Mandate

"That the generation to come might know them...and declare them to their children."

Children are leaving the faith at alarming rates. Years of surveys are confirming this. Church leaders and denominations are beginning to speak out. Multiple books on the subject are surfacing. And statistic after statistic is verifying the same ugly picture. We are losing our children. Even with all the evidence escalating, most of us do not need to see the numbers. More statistics are not required because the truth is right in front of us. Chances are that you know young people who have already walked away from the faith. Maybe you have seen it in your church. Maybe it has occurred within your own family.

My husband and I spent several years working in our church with the youth group before he became a full-time pastor. We invested five years of Bible study, fellowships, and counseling with this group. During that time, many made professions of faith and began walking with Christ. But they did not continue. Sadly, by the time they were out of high school, 90% of this group walked away from the church and their professed faith.

In our case, most of these children had parents who were unbelievers or not active in church. No doubt, this had to contribute to the outcome. However, those with unbelieving parents are not the only ones who are leaving. Many young people, raised by Christian parents and brought up in church, are walking away from their faith. Some walk away for a time; some of them never return. Then you have those who remained in practice, but long ago walked away in heart. I ashamedly admit that I was one of these children. I came to the faith at an early age, but spent years in rebellion to God. Thankful, the Lord lovingly drew me back, but the testimony remains of wasted years and regrets. Other factors to this departure include easy believism or the prosperity gospel that is so commonly producing false converts. Not understanding the need for repentance often results in those who "try" Jesus for a while without confessing and forsaking their sins (Proverbs 28:13). It could be that the reason many "leave the faith" is because they never had true faith to begin with. Who is to blame? How do we fix the problem? What is the churches role? And is there hope for our children? These questions need to be asked.

God ordained three institutions – family, government, and church. They are each separate with individual roles in society. When these institutions cross over in jurisdiction problems arise. The family is made up of husband, wife, and children. The parents are responsible for raising the children physically, mentally, emotionally, and spiritually. The government was ordained to be a *"minister to God,"* (Romans 13:1-7). Its primary responsibility is to protect those who do right and punish those who do wrong. The church is responsible for protecting, preserving, and propagating the gospel. This is done through edification and evangelism. Each are ordained by God, each are essential, and each are separate from one another.

So the question to ask is, just where does discipleship come in? Should our government disciple our children? Is it the responsibility of the church, or should it be left up to the parents? Most homeschooling families will undoubtedly declare that it is not the responsibility of the government to disciple or educate our children. The fact that we are homeschooling validates our beliefs. So we are left with the conclusion that either the church or the home is responsible. Given the title of this book, you have probably already recognized this author's belief. The discipleship of children belongs in the home, as you will soon see.

In order to understand Home Discipleship, we must first understand the meaning of the words disciple and discipleship.

Often when the word disciple is mentioned, the original twelve followers of Jesus come to mind. These were the students of Christ. He was their rabbi, master, or teacher. The idea of discipleship can be found in the Great Commission from Matthew 28:19-20. *"Go ye therefore, and teach..."* This word "teach" is μαθητεύω (mathēteuō) and means to disciple. Discipleship is the process by which a disciple is mentored to become more like their teacher. This is done by the student adhering to the teaching and doctrine taught. The ultimate goal of discipleship is that the disciple eventually assists in spreading the doctrine of their teacher to others.

When we understand this in light of the twelve it makes perfect sense. Jesus did not just teach these men; they spent three years of their life with him, day in and day out. He invested in them and poured His life into them. They followed him, literally. Then they took what they learned and began to teach others, who in turn taught others. The promulgation of the gospel is proof that they were true disciples. The process of making disciples has carried on throughout the centuries and will continue to do so until the end of the world. Jesus' promise was, *"Lo, I am with you alway, even unto the end of the world. Amen."*

Now, let's take this thought of discipleship into the home. As a pastor, my husband will remind his congregation that the home is often the most neglected mission field. We see the Great Commission as a church commission and rightly so. But because the church is an assembled people or congregation (and not just a place or building) it applies to every individual within the local church. As born again believers, we are all to be disciple makers. Not only are we commanded to make disciples, each of us are fully equipped at the moment of salvation. Therefore, the most logical starting place should be the home because the home is where our sphere of influence is the greatest.

It is important to understand that the influence we have as parents can be either good or bad, but either way it holds great weight. Let me be transparent for a moment; I must say that there are times that the thought of my children becoming just like me is terrifying. I have faults and failures that I do not want to pass along to my children. I want to pass on only the best things, but children see it all. They know us better than anyone else. They see us for who we really are. They know when we are genuine and when we are not. Children can tell if our faith is real. They can tell what is important to us by how we live. The old saying that "more is caught than taught" holds truth. We cannot give to our children what we do not possess. And even then, if we possess true faith, discipleship is not automatic. It takes sacrificial work.

Unfortunately, disciple making in the home is often thought of last, or sadly, not at all. For some reason we think that if we are believers our children will automatically come to Christ and follow His ways. This notion is dangerous. Discipleship must be a constant effort. I ashamedly admit that my husband and I have been guilty of investing time, money, and resources in the name of ministry, evangelism, and discipleship toward others only to neglect the discipleship of our own precious children. My children are pastor's kids so it seems as though they have spent more time at the church building than at home. And I am thankful that they see all the aspects of ministry and have active roles within, but we must remember that these things alone are not discipleship. While they certainly play a role, they are not the entirety of it. Thankfully, God is greater than any mistakes we make as parents. When my husband and I realize that we have neglected the discipleship of our children, our hearts desire is to repent and then refocus on the correct priorities.

There are many misconceptions about discipleship. The most common fallacy, as mentioned above, is that simply bringing children to church will suffice. One Sunday, after my husband preached a sermon on home discipleship, a man walked up to him and brashly exclaimed that discipleship does not work. He said, "I took my children to church every time the doors were open and look at them now! They are all living ungodly, wicked lives." My husband tried to explain the point of the sermon again to this man. "I did not say that taking your children to church was discipleship. I was referring to the actions in the home. Did you pray with your children? Did you read the Bible together as a family? Did you show them the fear of the Lord? Did you study doctrine together? Did you praise God and worship Him as a family? These are the things that constitute discipleship." Sadly, all this man could do was walk away.

I love the church. The church is *"the pillar and ground of the truth,"* 1 Timothy 3:15. Christ called His church (Matthew 4:18-21), Christ confirms His church (Matt 16:18), Christ loves and died for His church (Ephesians 5:25), and Christ will one day return for His church (1 Thessalonians 4:17). But, it is not the job of the church to disciple our children any more than it is the responsibility of the government to educate our children. As home educators we understand this. As Christian parents, we will be held accountable for the education of our children. And we, not the church, will be held accountable for the discipleship of our children. A true church following the dictate of Scripture will help equip parents to do the work of discipleship. Did you catch that? The church plays a role in discipleship; the church is to equip.

A church should not facilitate spiritual laziness by letting Christian parents abdicate their God-given role. But unfortunately, society as a whole leans towards parents relinquishing their authority over to others. It is common practice to turn our babies over to someone who gets paid to watch them at a very early age. When the children reach school age, the parents are then expected to turn them over to school officials for 30-40 hours a week. So it seems natural, for even Christian parents, to turn over their children's discipleship to the church. Many churches wrongly support this approach. They do so by making it easy for parents to drop off their children at the doors of the church. They do this by telling parents that the church will teach, train, and entertain the children. The attitude is "Just bring your children to church and we'll take care of the rest." But this has never been God's design for children being discipled in the faith. So why is it that when we disciple children man's way, instead of God's, do we then question the reason it is not working and they "leave the faith"?

We have seen in the New Testament the mandate for discipleship, but this mandate goes back even further than the first century. Long before the Great Commission was given to Christ's church, God's children were given the mandate to disciple their children within the home.

> *"Now these are the commandments, the statutes, and the judgments, which the LORD your God commanded to teach you, that ye might do them in the land whither ye go to possess it: That thou mightest fear the LORD thy God, to keep all his statutes and his commandments, which I command thee, thou, and thy son, and thy son's son, all the days of thy life; and that thy days may be prolonged. Hear therefore, O Israel, and observe to do it; that it may be well with thee, and that ye may increase mightily, as the LORD God of thy fathers hath promised thee, in the land that floweth with milk and honey. Hear, O Israel: The LORD our God is one LORD: And thou shalt love the LORD thy God with all thine heart, and with all thy soul, and with all thy might. And these words, which I command thee this day, shall be in thine heart: And thou shalt teach them diligently unto thy children, and shalt talk of them when thou sittest in thine house, and when thou walkest by the*

way, and when thou liest down, and when thou risest up." Deuteronomy 6:1-7

Just as the Shema is applicable for today, so is the command to *"teach them diligently unto thy children."* As we see here in this passage, discipleship is an ongoing transformation that occurs all the time (in your house, as you walk throughout the day, when you go to bed, and when you get up). Homeschooling parents have a distinct advantage in this area. We are with our children most of the day and are given more opportunities to teach and train. And just as Christ's teachings were spread throughout the world by His disciples, we are to impart this teaching to our children with a multi-generational vision. *"That the generation to come might know them, even the children which should be born; who should arise and declare them to their children,"* Psalm 78:6.

There is a biblical mandate for Home Discipleship. It is set before you, the Christian parent. Will you rise to the challenge? Throughout the rest of this book we will look at how we can effectively and practically disciple our children in knowledge, wisdom, and the ways of the Lord. And we will address how a homeschooling lifestyle can help parents accomplish this very objective.

Practical Application

1. We cannot pass on to our children what we do not possess. Do you know without a doubt that you are in the faith? Second Corinthians 13:5a says, *"Examine yourselves, whether ye be in the faith; prove your own selves."*

2. Have you believed the lie that just bringing children to church is good enough for discipleship?

3. We are to teach our children diligently. Look up the definition of diligent. What does diligent teaching look like in your home? Do you believe that you are teaching your children the things of the Lord in this manner?

4. If you are not discipling your children, do you feel led to begin true discipleship? What can you implement in the home starting today? If you are actively pursuing the discipleship of your children, how can you improve upon the discipleship activities you are currently doing?

5. The true goal of discipleship is that those who are discipled will begin to disciple others. Are you giving your saved children service opportunities and teaching them to share and defend their faith?

Chapter 2
The Structure Of The Home

"If the foundations be destroyed, what can the righteous do?"

Every worthwhile structure needs to be built on a firm foundation and the Christian home is no different. Before the discipleship process in our children can even begin, we need to make sure that the foundation of the home is solid and sure. Jesus Christ is the foundation of a Christian home. Upon that foundation we build our family. My husband and I have counseled with many Christian homeschooling families who are falling apart. They might appear to be healthy and striving as a family, but it is just a façade. They have the foundation of Christ in their home, but they are building a weak, unsecured structure upon that foundation. Our enemy, the great deceiver, is seeking to destroy Christian families. If Christ is truly the foundation of the home, we rest in the peace that the foundation cannot be destroyed. But this does not keep the enemy from seeking to tear down the framework of the home.

The framework of the Christian home is the marriage. Think about what happens when Christian marriages are destroyed. The home is shattered, churches are weakened, testimonies are lost, and the enemy is victorious when this occurs. This is because the biblical marriage on earth is a representation of the perfect heavenly marriage. We find this truth in Ephesians 5:22-32.

> *"Wives, submit yourselves unto your own husbands, as unto the Lord. For the husband is the head of the wife, even as Christ is the head of the church: and he is the saviour of the body. Therefore as the church is subject unto Christ, so let the wives be to their own husbands in every thing. Husbands, love your wives, even as Christ also loved the church, and gave himself for it; That he might sanctify and cleanse it with the washing of water by the word, That he might present it to himself a glorious church, not having spot, or wrinkle, or any such thing; but that it should be holy and without blemish. So ought men to love their wives as their own bodies. He that loveth his wife loveth himself. For no man ever yet hated his own flesh; but nourisheth and cherisheth it, even as the Lord the church: For we are*

> *members of his body, of his flesh, and of his bones. For this cause shall a man leave his father and mother, and shall be joined unto his wife, and they two shall be one flesh. This is a great mystery: but I speak concerning Christ and the church."*

When Christian marriages operate in an unbiblical fashion, they portray to the world a distorted and false view of Christ and His bride. It is true that many couples do not think about their marriage in this light. Problems become blinding, and too many times people are so busy focusing on themselves that their testimony to the world is not even considered. But bearing in mind the current state of marriage within the Christian community, it is high time that Christian people start thinking about these things. What is your marriage saying to those around you? As children of God, does your marriage reflect the power of God in your life? When the unsaved world looks at your marriage are they drawn to God and His glorious truths? Our testimony makes it imperative for Christian couples to focus on building a strong marriage based on the Word of God.

The Christian marriage is not about "me" or even "we". It is all about "He"! Wives are to submit to their husbands *"as unto the Lord."* It is all about Him! Husbands are to love their wives, *"even as Christ also loved the church, and gave himself for it."* Again, it is all about Him! When we view our marriage in light of the testimony we are giving to the unsaved world, it greatly motivates us to have a God-pleasing marriage.

Not only is building a strong marriage a vital part of our testimony, but it is a fundamental part of the discipleship of our children. Psalm 127 describes our objective as Christian parents.

> *"Except the LORD build the house, they labour in vain that build it: except the LORD keep the city, the watchman waketh but in vain. It is vain for you to rise up early, to sit up late, to eat the bread of sorrows: for so he giveth his beloved sleep. Lo, children are an heritage of the LORD: and the fruit of the womb is his reward. As arrows are in the hand of a mighty man; so are children of the youth. Happy is the man that hath his quiver full of them: they shall not be ashamed, but they shall speak with the enemies in the gate."*

"Except the LORD build the house…" Notice again that the foundation of the home is Christ. In verse three the Psalmist declares, *"Lo, children are an heritage of the LORD: and the fruit of the womb is his reward."* They are a direct blessing from God. He gives them to us to bring up in nurture and admonition of the Lord (Ephesians 6:4). Part of bringing them up is *"teach them diligently"* as discussed in the previous chapter. We bring them up and we teach them diligently so that one day we can send them out. We see this principle when God instituted the family in Genesis chapter two. *"Therefore shall a man leave his father and his*

mother, and shall cleave unto his wife: and they shall be one flesh," Genesis 2:24. My husband and I greatly desire to one day send our children out of our home so that they can leave, cleave, and weave a life with their spouse. When we send them out, we send them into the world as a warrior would fly arrows toward the enemy. *"As arrows are in the hand of a mighty man; so are children of the youth,"* Psalm 127:4.

As the passage continues we are again reminded of the blessings associated with having children. *"Happy is the man that hath his quiver full of them,"* Psalm 127:5a. They are a blessing to not only us, but to the world as well. Notice that there is a sense of protection associated with sending out spiritually strong children *"...they shall not be ashamed, but they shall speak with the enemies in the gate,"* Psalm 127:5b. Christians are becoming a minority in this nation. We are surrounded by enemies who wish to destroy biblical homes and every Christian value. Our nation is in dire need of young Christians who are spiritually strong. Therefore, we have quite a job to do as parents. It will take a multi-generational vision to turn our nation around. It will take one family at a time doing the work. And it will take strong marriages, built on the foundation of Christ, to accomplish all we are called to do.

Every Christian family wants the blessings of God upon their home. Look at how the Psalmist describes the blessed man in the very next Psalm.

"Blessed is every one that feareth the LORD; that walketh in his ways. For thou shalt eat the labour of thine hands: happy shalt thou be, and it shall be well with thee. Thy wife shall be as a fruitful vine by the sides of thine house: thy children like olive plants round about thy table. Behold, that thus shall the man be blessed that feareth the LORD. The LORD shall bless thee out of Zion: and thou shalt see the good of Jerusalem all the days of thy life. Yea, thou shalt see thy children's children, and peace upon Israel."
Psalm 128

The blessed man is described as one that *"feareth the Lord"* and *"walketh in his ways"*. The secret of blessing is living in reverent obedience to God. We must build our families as God intended. It will not be easy; in fact, it will be very difficult to live in obedience to Christ. The enemy is against us; the world is against us; and our own weak flesh battles against us. But in Christ we are victorious!

- He has already overcome the enemy.

"And the devil that deceived them was cast into the lake of fire and brimstone, where the beast and the false prophet are, and shall be tormented day and night for ever and ever," Revelation 20:10.

- Those that are born of God have overcome the world.

"For whatsoever is born of God overcometh the world: and this is the victory that overcometh the world, even our faith," 1 John 5:4.

- Even our flesh has been defeated.

"Knowing this, that our old man is crucified with him, that the body of sin might be destroyed, that henceforth we should not serve sin," Romans 6:6.

Although it is hard to live in obedience, it is certainly not impossible for the believer.

Once this foundation is set and the proper framework built, then a family can add academics into the structure of the home. Remember that academic excellence is a commendable goal, but it must be properly laid with the correct foundation.

"For other foundation can no man lay than that is laid, which is Jesus Christ. Now if any man build upon this foundation gold, silver, precious stones, wood, hay, stubble; Every man's work shall be made manifest: for the day shall declare it, because it shall be revealed by fire; and the fire shall try every man's work of what sort it is. If any man's work abide which he hath built thereupon, he shall receive a reward." 1 Corinthians 3:11-14

Think of the parents as the builders, God as the architect, and His Word as the blueprints needed to build a Christian home. The sure foundation is Jesus Christ and the gold, silver, and precious stones are those things that are of eternal value. In the end nothing else will matter. When the fiery trials of life come and when all our works are manifested, we want to know that what we have built into our homes, marriage, and children will last.

Practical Application

1. Christ is the foundation of the Christian home and the marriage is the framework that is built upon that foundation. In construction we know that the foundation is the most important aspect, but once it has been laid how important is it to use the best materials possible and the proper methods when building a structure?

2. Just as you would never add the walls to a house before framing it in, neither should the children of the home come before the marriage. A healthy home is not "child-centered." If the children are the focus, what happens when they leave?

3. While it is not intentional, it is easy to place building a strong, biblical marriage at the bottom of the priority list. What are some things you can do this week to strengthen your marriage?

4. The enemy is seeking to destroy Christian families. It is also safe to say that Christian families who have chosen to homeschool their children are an even bigger target. Look up 1 Corinthians 10:12. How does this apply to our homes?

5. (Wife) Proverbs 14:1 says, *"Every wise woman buildeth her house: but the foolish plucketh it down with her hands."* In what ways have you plucked down your home? In what ways have you built it up?

6. (Husband) In Scripture we see the father's role as physical and spiritual leader of the family. Look up and study the following passages this week: Genesis 3:1-9, Genesis 35:1-5, Deuteronomy 6:1-2, Joshua 4:20-24, Ephesians 5:23-33.

Chapter 3
The Proper Perspective

"Teach us to number our days, that we may apply our hearts unto wisdom."

Through His Word, God has given us the knowledge necessary for the discipleship of our children. However, if knowledge was enough for success, many Christian homes would look drastically different. True success will involve having wisdom in that we can apply these principles to our life. But we are not to have just any type of wisdom, for James chapter three tells of two types.

> *"Who is a wise man and endued with knowledge among you? let him shew out of a good conversation his works with meekness of wisdom. But if ye have bitter envying and strife in your hearts, glory not, and lie not against the truth. This wisdom descendeth not from above, but is earthly, sensual, devilish. For where envying and strife is, there is confusion and every evil work. But the wisdom that is from above is first pure, then peaceable, gentle, and easy to be intreated, full of mercy and good fruits, without partiality, and without hypocrisy."* James 3:13-17

There is earthly wisdom and there is heavenly wisdom. Sadly, many Christians function with earthly wisdom. I certainly have from time to time. Yet, every time I seek the world's wisdom it produces strife in my heart and ultimately my life.

Heavenly wisdom comes from God and Him alone (Proverbs 2:6). Seeking it should be our hearts desire (Proverbs 4:7). It is better than rubies (Proverbs 8:11), fine gold, and silver (Proverbs 3:13-14). The beginning of it is fear of the Lord. *"Give instruction to a wise man, and he will be yet wiser: teach a just man, and he will increase in learning. The fear of the LORD is the beginning of wisdom: and the knowledge of the holy is understanding,"* Proverbs 9:9-10. Just what does it mean to have "fear of the Lord"? Fear usually denotes a negative connotation in our minds, but this fear is not one that brings torment. The fear of the Lord is a filial, reverential, holy fear. It is motivated by a love for God, an understanding of who He is, and an awe of Him.

The Bible speaks a lot about having wisdom. We all need it. We will particularly need wisdom in regards to discipling our children. Wisdom will also help us keep our priorities in the proper perspective. We all know from experience that life can become busy. Being too busy will hinder our family more than perhaps any other thing. When this happens, it becomes easy to go through the motions of being a Christian, a husband or wife, a parent, or even homeschooling our children. But discipleship is not about going through the motions. It cannot be. Discipleship is an investment that takes a lot of time and a proper perspective.

Have you ever met a person who at the end of their life said, "I sure wish I had not wasted my life by spending so much time with my family?" Usually the direct opposite is voiced. With regret in their voice we hear phrases like:

- "I've spent my entire life focusing on my work. Now that work is gone so is my family."

- "I've neglected my wife and children all these years."

- "I was always too busy to tell my parents just how much I loved them, now it's too late."

- "Life was hectic. I never took the time to stop and talk with my children. Now they won't talk to me."

- "My parents never read the Bible or prayed with me. That was something we only did at church."

- "I was so busy teaching my children math and science that I never took time to enjoy them."

Tempus Fugit. In Latin it means, time flies. Oh, how true it is. Just yesterday I was holding my beloved's hand and saying, "I do and I will till death do us part." Now, twenty years later I ask myself, where has the time gone? It seems as though just yesterday I was holding my first born in my arms, singing sweet songs, and rocking him to sleep. Now, sixteen years later and towering over six feet tall, he could rock me. Where did the time go? Just yesterday I was opening that first box of homeschool books as we began our journey to home educate our children. Now, the path is well worn and I'm looking back over years of discipleship with my children. There are just a few years left. Again, where has the time gone? I know in my heart that years from now I will be looking back at even this season in my life and asking the all too familiar question of where did the time go?

The Lord answers our question. In Psalms we are told why time flies so quickly. *"My days are like a shadow that declineth; and I am withered like grass,"* Psalm 102:11. Life is short and the time we are given to disciple our children is even shorter. Therefore, I should be as the Psalmist and *"remember how short my time is,"* Psalm 89:47. In the book of James we are reminded again just how short life is. *"Whereas ye know not what shall be on the morrow. For what is your life? It is even a vapour, that appeareth for a little time, and then vanisheth away,"* James 4:14.

When my children were younger, I would teach them science lessons about the three stages of water. We would fill a glass with water to show the liquid state. We would put a cup of water in the freezer so it could freeze. Then we would put a cup of water on the stove to watch it evaporate. As we watched the steam rise, one reoccurring thought was that it vanishes so quickly. And while that is true, when steam (or vapor) is channeled properly it can be put to great work.

Consider the steam engine. Steam engines were the first widespread engine type to be used. They were the foundation of the industrial revolution. They powered all early locomotives, steam boats, and factories. Even today we see that steam is one of the most widely used commodities for conveying heat energy. Because water is plentiful and inexpensive, steam is efficient and economic to generate. Now consider this. Our lives are but a vapor; they appear for a little while and then vanish away. Consequently, our lives can be wasted and allowed to drift aimlessly like a vapor in the air until they are gone or, if allowed to, they can be channeled properly by the Holy Spirit and accomplish great things for God while here on earth.

So, in reply to tempus fugit I will say to the Lord as the Psalmist did to, *"teach us to number our days, that we may apply our hearts unto wisdom,"* Psalm 90:12. A good understanding of our own frailty and shortness of life should move us to live in wisdom. In answer to the question of where time has gone, I will say that it has gone to afternoons of walking hand in hand with my husband. It has gone to playing a board game with my children. It has gone to holding my children on my lap and reading story after story. It has gone to baking cookies with my daughter to take to a lonely widow. It has gone to hours and hours of teaching my children math, science, and history. It has gone to daily Bible instruction as we all learn together the ways of God more perfectly. It has gone to smiling, laughing, and giggling with my family. It has gone to singing old hymns around the piano. And so much more.

But, time has also been given to days of sadness, frustration, anger, and worry. Time has gone to fighting and an unforgiving heart. Time has been given to futile projects and lessons of little substance. Time has been wasted on frivolous actions that will never matter in eternity. Time has been given over to selfishness more times than I care to count. Time has been wasted. If not careful we will allow our lives to be bombarded with meaningless activity that rob us of our precious time. We must close our ears to the wisdom of this world. It whispers lies that bog us down with trifle doings.

The following quote by David Breese, from Living For Eternity, is one of my favorites. It is framed and hung on my husband's office wall.

"Strong sons of God are not perfected by childish pursuits."

How many Christians go through life pursuing childish things of this world? I know that our family is guilty at times. Life is short, so we cannot afford to waste it. What are you doing with the short time you have been given? Is your life channeled properly by the Holy Spirit and accomplishing great things for God? Are your priorities in check? Is having a God honoring marriage a priority in our life? Is discipling your children a priority?

We need heavenly wisdom to help us keep the proper perspective on the things that really matter in life. Without it we will easily become side tracked. Remember, this wisdom is *"pure, peaceable, gentle, easy to be intreated, full of mercy and good fruits, without partiality, and without hypocrisy"*. Do you need some? All you have to do is ask. *"If any of you lack wisdom, let him ask of God,"* James 1:5a.

Practical Application

1. The book of Proverbs speaks a lot about the parent's role in teaching wisdom to the children. *"My son, hear the instruction of thy father, and forsake not the law of thy mother,"* Proverbs 1:8. Commit as a family to read and study one chapter of Proverbs each day.

2. Have you ever felt like you are just going through the motions in life? Recognizing the problem is the first step in fixing it. What areas of your life does this occur most often (work, your marriage, as a parent, or as a homeschooling family)?

3. Consider doing a unit study on steam with your children. Tie in the thought from James 4:14 about our life being a vapor.

4. How we spend our time can be an indication of our priorities in life. Take time to document how your time is spent in an average week.

5. The quote, *"Strong sons of God are not perfected by childish pursuits"* is a great reminder. What "childish pursuits" have you chased after individually and as a family?

Chapter 4
The Higher Education

"For as the heavens are higher than the earth, so are my ways higher than your ways,"

As a homeschooling parent, the day comes when you realize that it is time to move past reading and phonics and onto reports and essays. A time comes when we stop teaching addition and subtraction and begin to teach about polynomials and quadratic equations. Some children will even surpass learning about certain sciences, such as biology, and begin to discover chemical equations or maybe even Stoichiometry. As home educators, we take this journey, one step at a time, to lead our children down the path to what society considers higher education. But there is a higher education still and, as said before, it is much more than ABC's and 123's. It is much more than the attainment of knowledge. This higher education is attained through discipleship. Regardless of the age of children or where they are academically, we should be diligent in guiding them towards this higher education. In fact, we should all strive to continue in it. It is not so much instruction for the mind, but for the soul. It is not higher in academics, but in wisdom. It is not elevated by man's standards, but by God's. It is not achieved through the study of text books, but by learning and meditating upon God's Word. The higher education is the one that is able to make man wise unto salvation through faith in Christ Jesus. It comes from the Holy Scriptures and is given to us *"for doctrine, for reproof, for correction, for instruction in righteousness,"* 2 Timothy 3:16.

To know God and to learn of Him is the best education we will ever give our children. Academics fade in comparison to the light of His Glory. Some would read into this that I do not put any stock into my children's education, but nothing could be further from the truth. One of the reasons we homeschool is so that our children will have a good, solid, biblical education. We are called to be good stewards and that includes the use of our minds. But, our number one goal as Christian parents should be seeking the *higher* education for our children.

Let me explain it like this: Jesus once told his disciples, *"If any man come to me, and hate not his father, and mother, and wife, and children, and brethren, and sisters, yea, and his own life also, he cannot be my disciple,"* Luke 14:26. Was Jesus telling us to hate our family? Of course not! What He was saying is that the love we have for Him should be so deep and so high that, in comparison, the love we have for our family *seems* like hatred. That is what I am trying to illustrate about educating our children. The higher, most preeminent things should be of God, His Word, and His Son. In comparison, everything else *seems* insignificant.

In speaking through the Prophet Isaiah, the Lord said, *"For as the heavens are higher than the earth, so are my ways higher than your ways, and my thoughts than your thoughts,"* Isaiah 55:9. God's ways are always higher. So as a Christian, it is already established in my heart that I should be teaching my children the higher things of God – this higher education, if you will.

I can certainly appreciate the words of the Apostle Paul. In Philippians 3:12 he stated, *"Not as though I had already attained, either were already perfect."* You see, we are far from perfect. We have not yet attained. We fail often. As parents, we want to do right, but we do not have all the answers. There is, however, One who does have all the answers. There is One who is perfect, Jesus Christ. He never fails. He guides our family with His precious Word. He leads us down paths of righteousness for His name's sake. He goes before us and behind us and lays His hand upon us. And as my husband follows Him, the children and I follow my husband. We are not perfect, but we strive to *"press toward the mark for the prize of the high calling of God in Christ Jesus,"*

Philippians 3:14. Is that your desire as a family?

Seeking God is first in the pursuit of leading our children toward a higher education. *"O God, thou art my God; early will I seek thee,"* Psalm 63:1a. Notice that Psalms 63:1 says, *"early will I seek thee"*. It does not say early will I read my Bible nor early will I write in my prayer journal. It says I will seek *thee*. It will be hard to teach our children how to seek God if we do not properly seek Him ourselves. It is more than casually reading the Bible. It is more than saying a prayer. It is to seek His face and to know His presence. Of course, the quantity of time we spend in prayer, communicating with our Lord, greatly affects our relationship. I long for this, for myself and for my children.

While seeking God is more than Bible study, the study of God's Word is an important part of it. Because of its significance, Bible study is something we will address all throughout this book. The Bible should be a part of our children's education, but we must be very careful in how we approach the study of God's Word. There have been times when we went through our daily Bible lessons hurrying just to finish. I am sure many parents can relate. And while this approach is not good for any subject, how much worse is it to treat the things of God flippantly? The study of God's Word should be something we hold in high esteem to our children.

Remember that even studying the Bible can be a heart issue. I never wanted a Bible lesson to be the only biblical teaching my children received throughout the day. I desire for my children to learn God's principles all day (Deuteronomy 6:7); over breakfast, in every subject, while they played, while they worked, and when they went to bed. God should not be something we add onto a busy schedule; He should be the very center of our lives.

If you choose to use a Bible curriculum, each family must evaluate what type to use. There are many great resources for parents. We have used various curriculums over the years, but have come to the conclusion that expository (verse-by-verse) Bible study is the best way to learn, especially for older children. We believe the Bible is clear on how to study Scriptures and grow in knowledge. *"Whom shall he teach knowledge? and whom shall he make to understand doctrine? ... For precept must be upon precept, precept upon precept; line upon line, line upon line; here a little, and there a little,"* Isaiah 28:9-10. Scripture should be studied in context; precept upon precept, line upon line.

The most common mistake made in studying the Bible is taking verses out of context. Text without context is pretext. When Scripture is taken out of context it is easy to have preconceived notions about what the text means. It is easy to twist verses taken out of context and embrace false ideas. For that reason, expository study is best in order to fully understand the truths of God.

In addition to seeking God and studying His Word, Bible memorization can play a role in guiding our children toward a higher education. I do not know if my children will memorize all the Periodic Table of Elements and their atomic numbers. I do not even know if that will be a priority in their education. But a top priority is that they learn to hide God's Word in their hearts. *"Thy word have I hid in mine heart, that I might not sin against thee,"* Psalms 119:11. What a precious gift to give your children! I realize that here in America there is a Bible everywhere we turn. Many people have them on their computers and on their phones. If we need to know God's Word we can simply look it up. But will we always have this privilege? Will there be a time when the only Word we have is what we have hidden in our hearts? What about when a decision must be made and there is no time to look into God's Word? But if we will memorize the Word of God it will always be with us. If we teach our children to memorize God's Word, they too will always have it.

There are many ways to incorporate Bible memorization into your daily life with your children. Our family makes a point to place Scripture throughout the house. It does not have to be expensive or elaborate artwork. With a printer and ordinary frames, you can add beautiful Scripture verses to every room of your home. One of our favorite pieces of art is a wooden frame, made by a homeschooling father and his boys, with the inscription "Write Them on the Doorpost". It holds up to ten 8x10 sheets of cardstock. On each piece of paper is a different section of Scripture that we want the children to memorize. The frame hangs by our dining room table. During dinner my husband reads the Scripture we are working on to the children and they repeat it back to him. When everyone in the family memorizes that section we pull out a new one to work on.

A father's leadership is vital to the spiritual growth of a

family. This is the way God planned it. As wives we should encourage and support our husbands in this leading. But wife, if your husband is not leading spiritually, be very careful in how you approach him. No man's heart has ever been changed by a nagging wife. God's instructions for winning a husband are through a meek and quiet spirit.

> *"Likewise, ye wives, be in subjection to your own husbands; that, if any obey not the word, they also may without the word be won by the conversation of the wives; While they behold your chaste conversation coupled with fear. Whose adorning let it not be that outward adorning of plaiting the hair, and of wearing of gold, or of putting on of apparel; But let it be the hidden man of the heart, in that which is not corruptible, even the ornament of a meek and quiet spirit, which is in the sight of God of great price,"* 1 Peter 3:1-4.

If a husband is not obeying the word of God by leading his family spiritually, the wife has the power to change his heart through her behavior. God sees a meek and quiet spirit as a precious treasure, and so will a husband.

There is another aspect of a higher education. We are to seek God through prayer, study His word, and memorize His word, but we are also to meditate upon His word. As a very young child I memorized the 23rd Psalm. If someone asked me to recite it, I could repeat it perfectly. But as a small child, I did not fully understand the passage. To show to what extent my young mind erred, I thought that when the psalmist said, *"The Lord is my shepherd; I shall not want,"* that the psalmist did not want the shepherd. I did not understand that the phrase *"I shall not want"* meant that because the Lord is the Shepherd we are never in need. It is amusing now to think how my young mind thought, but it proves a point. A person can memorize something without fully understanding it. When we mediate upon God's Word we take what we have put into our mind and we put it into our heart. It is gaining knowledge and wisdom. It is deeply comprehending what we are memorizing and applying it to our lives. When we memorize, we study. When we meditate, we reflect.

The benefits of seeking a higher education for your children are untold. Your family will be drawn closer together as each of you draws closer to the Lord. We are talking about spiritual implications that are everlasting. We will never know this side of eternity what impact we made on our children and what impact they made on others. Is it difficult to seek the higher things? Yes, it will be. Is it worth the effort? Absolutely!

Practical Application

1. Prayer is a vital part of seeking God. By what process are you teaching your children how to pray?

2. Is Bible study something you do as a family, as part of your children's schooling, or both? Do you need to re-evaluate how you study the Bible as a family?

3. Is memorizing the Scriptures and meditating upon them a priority in your children's life? Is it a priority in your life? What family activities can you do to encourage both?

4. Second Timothy 3:16 says, *"All scripture is given by inspiration of God, and is profitable for doctrine, for reproof, for correction, for instruction in righteousness."* In simple terms the Scriptures tell us the things that are right (doctrine), the things that are wrong (reproof), how to get right (correction), and how to stay right (instruction). Look up the definition of the word "profitable" and study this verse as a family.

5. Read Philippians 3:10-14. What is the *"high calling"* that Paul is referring to? How is it accomplished?

Chapter 5
The Fundamentals

"Children, obey your parents in all things: for this is well pleasing unto the Lord."

Discipleship is an ongoing process. It takes years to instill in children the values and principles that need to be taught. From the time children are born, they are being influenced in how they think and what they believe. Sometimes this influence is more negative than positive. After all, not all parents start out on the right path. It has taken my husband and me years of following Christ and studying the Scriptures to even understand the importance of true discipleship. While we know we are on the correct path, we still have a long way to travel. The key, however, is staying on the path and moving forward – or in other words – striving.

In addition to the discipleship process, we strive to give our children the best education possible. And like discipleship, a good education will not automatically happen. It takes work, and lots of it. We made the choice to educate our children at home when our first child was just 4 years old. We have adjusted to this lifestyle slowly, one child at a time. And believe me when I tell you, it is a lifestyle, especially when discipleship is the ultimate goal.

But not all families are able to adjust incrementally. Several years ago we were at a Mississippi Homeschooling Conference and met a sweet couple at a local coffee bar. They were just about to embark on their first year of homeschooling. The father was recently saved and as a result his family was drastically changing. They had adult children who had not grown up in the faith, and they desperately wanted to make sure the younger ones would. So, they made the decision to take them out of school and begin to homeschool. They were at the conference to seek wisdom. A significant transformation was happening in this family and it was quite overwhelming. Therefore, they faced a few challenges and had a lot of questions.

As the homeschool movement grows, more and more families are opting out of traditional school for their children and bringing them home. Fathers are stepping out in faith and leading their family in this area. Mothers are learning how to make the adjustment to homeschool their children. They have embarked on a grand adventure and life has now changed. Their children have spent several years in the public system and now they too have to adjust. Suddenly, the rules have changed. The environment, the teacher, their peers, and curriculum have changed. In other words, everything in their life has changed.

There is one question that is often asked by new homeschooling parents. "How do I go from being my child's parent to now becoming my child's teacher?" My answer is simply that you do not go from parent to teacher. You become a teaching parent. Your children need a parent more than anything. No person loves them more than you do and no one has a more vested interest in their education than you.

When children come home there is one imperative lesson that must be taught first. Until this lesson is taught and achieved, you should not move forward. Regardless of age, children must first learn to obey and honor their parents. Ephesians 6:1-3 says, *"Children, obey your parents in the Lord: for this is right. Honour thy father and mother; (which is the first commandment with promise;) that it may be well with thee, and thou mayest live long on the earth."* This is the only command found in Scripture for children. It might sound simplistic, but it is the foundation upon which successful teaching is built. The parents' authority is given over to others when a child is placed outside the home. So, when that child comes home, the parents must now reestablish their parental authority. If this is not done, all teaching will be in vain.

Parents who have had their children at home with them since birth have a slight advantage in this area. They have had years to establish this principle. The children are always with them which lends to consistency in child training. This is, however, not always the case. Sometimes even veteran homeschooling parents need to address this issue and get back to the fundamentals of obedience.

Ephesians 6 gives two commands for children. They are to obey and honor. Obedience is an action. When you tell your daughter to sit still and write her spelling words, as she does exactly that, she is obedient. She does not get up and she completes her work. Honoring is different. It is an attitude. Not only does your daughter obey, but she does it with a right heart. She does not question, talk back, or roll her eyes. She obeys with a sweet spirit. This is honoring.

Shortly after we were first married, my husband brought home a Cocker Spaniel puppy named Jesse. This pup was out of control, so we decided to take him to obedience school. One of the first things the instructor taught us was that when we gave a command to only say it once. If you said, "Sit, Sit, SIT!!!!!" you would be training the dog to *not* obey at the first command. Since having children, I have learned a few things. First, children are much smarter than animals. If a dog can be trained to sit, stay, and speak with the smallest of commands, how much more should we expect intelligent children created in the image of God to be able to obey a simple command from their parents? Therefore, I have learned that the obedience of children will solely depend upon their training. Unfortunately, I have also learned that it is much harder to retrain a child than to properly train them from the beginning.

Part of teaching our children obedience is to teach them attentiveness. They must learn to listen if they are to obey. Have you ever caught yourself saying these things?

"Listen to me!"
"Are you paying attention?"
"Have you heard what I just said?"

One day when I was trying to teach my son the importance of being attentive, I took him to Proverbs 4:20-21, *"My son, attend to my words; incline thine ear unto my sayings. Let them not depart from thine eyes; keep them in the midst of thine heart."* I explained that being attentive means to listen with your ears, with your eyes, and with your heart. "How do you listen with your eyes?" He asked. "Well, Andrew," I said, "there are times when you can just look at Mommy and know what I want you to do without me even saying a word. And, son, without putting that knowledge in your heart, you are not really paying attention. If you do not pay attention, you will not be able to properly obey."

There is a great lesson here for parents as well. You see, it is very hard to teach principles that we do not adhere to. Since I am but a child and my Heavenly Father desires my obedience and attentiveness, I have tried to apply these truths to my life as well.

How many times does the Lord have to say to me, "Listen to me", "Are you paying attention?" or "Have you heard what I just said?" Too many times I am afraid. So I am learning to pay close attention to my Father and listen to the Words He has to say so that I can live in obedience. Part of honoring my Father is to listen to Him with my eyes. Psalm 32:8-9 says, *"I will instruct thee and teach thee in the way which thou shalt go: I will guide thee with mine eye. Be ye not as the horse, or as the mule, which have no understanding: whose mouth must be held in with bit and bridle, lest they come near unto thee."* In other words, do not be like an animal that must have incentive to come to their master. Do not be like the out of control puppy that is trained to expect a treat. Be the obedient child that gazes upon the Father and willingly and joyfully attends to His words. I know that when my eyes are fixed upon my Lord, all He has to do is nod His head to get my attention. He does not have to say a word because His Word is already hid in my heart. When we understand and apply attentiveness, obedience, and honor in our lives toward our Heavenly Father, it makes teaching the same principles to our children a little easier.

It is to the detriment of our children if we fail to teach them this fundamental lesson. A child who does not learn to consistently obey their parents will struggle in life. It will not go well with them (Ephesians 6:3). They will also struggle in their academic studies if obedience is a problem. But even more important than that, if we fail to teach our children to honor and obey us, they will not learn how to honor and obey God. A lack of proper respect and obedience for those in authority will transcend into a lack of proper respect and obedience for the Highest Authority – God Almighty.

When a parent first begins to teach, or when children who have been in a public school setting come home, there are a lot of expectations placed upon the parent. Sometimes these expectations come from outside sources and sometimes we place them upon ourselves. Most parents feel like they must prove something. This is normal. We want to jump right in and make sure our children are learning and excelling in their studies. But the fundamental principle of obedience is so important to the wellbeing and peace in a home that it must be established first. If it takes a week, two weeks, or even a month to properly train your children to honor and obey you, it is okay. If you need to put everything on hold for a short time to focus on this lesson, it is okay as well. If you need to go back and re-teach the same lesson over and over again, do it! In our family we have had to re-teach this fundamental lesson on many occasions. Reestablish proper authority in their lives and then point them to the Highest Authority. Obedience is a key part of discipleship. We are to build upon it so we can then successfully move on to other areas of study.

Practical Application

1. Ephesians 6:3 gives two promises for children who do this. What are they? Make a point to share these promises with your children this week.

2. It is hard to teach principles to our children that we, as parents, do not adhere to ourselves. Can we say that we are living a life of honor and obedience to our Heavenly Father?

3. Look up Psalm 71:8 and Revelation 4:11. Honoring is an attitude. In what ways can and should our family show honor to the Lord?

4. Look up Deuteronomy 13:4, John 14:15, and I John 2:3. Obedience is an action. In what ways can and should our family obey the Lord?

5. "A lack of proper respect and obedience for those in authority will transcend into a lack of proper respect and obedience for the Highest Authority – God Almighty." When we understand this principle, teaching our children to honor and obey us takes on a whole different connotation. In what ways does this thought motivate you to teach your children to honor and obey?

Chapter 6
The Standards & Goals

"Set your affection on things above, not on things on the earth."

"Mom, who is Oprah Winfrey?" my son asked one day sitting at the kitchen table. The state we lived in required standardized testing for 3rd through 9th grade. My son, then 8 years old, was reviewing a practice booklet when he asked the question. After explaining to him that she was a TV celebrity he asked, "Why do I need to know that?" With a smile in my heart I replied, "You don't." Later that evening I showed the book to my husband and pointed out several points of concern. After looking over the questions, we came to the conclusion that since the tests were from a secular, humanist, and evolutionary point-of-view, our son would simply be at a disadvantage in taking them. "Sweetheart, don't worry about it." My husband said. "After all, do we really want our children to be standardized?"

This is the very question we have asked every year since. As Christian parents do we want our children to be like the rest of the world? Unfortunately, it is a very easy trap to fall into. We have a vested interest in our children and want the best for them. So we ask the question, "What is best?" Many would agree that if children excel in academics, are well rounded in their social development, are active in sports, can play a musical instrument, are learning a foreign language, score high on the ACT, get a scholarship into a good college, and go on to make a high-paying career for themselves that they are successful. While the world would unquestionably view this as success, as a believer in Christ, these are not necessarily my standards. The Apostle John wrote in 1 John 2:15-17, *"Love not the world, neither the things that are in the world. If any man love the world, the love of the Father is not in him. For all that is in the world, the lust of the flesh, and the lust of the eyes, and the pride of life, is not of the Father, but is of the world. And the world passeth away, and the lust thereof: but he that doeth the will of God abideth for ever."* If we are not careful, our families will indulge in and love the things of this world. This kind of love is to our detriment, for there is a world system that we are not to love or cling to. The world will pass away therefore the way we live and the standards we set for our children need to be with eternity in mind. Otherwise, we have sold our children short, *"For what is a man advantaged, if he gain the whole world, and lose himself, or be cast away?"* Luke 9:25.

Is it wrong to want our children to excel in academics? Absolutely not! But if academic excellence is the goal without the foundation of God and His Word then our priorities are misplaced. *"If ye then be risen with Christ, seek those things which are above, where Christ sitteth on the right hand of God. Set your affection on things above, not on things on the earth,"* Colossians 3:1- 2. While I want my children to do well in their educational pursuit, I want to measure their success by God's standards and not the worlds. Everything that is passed through their minds need to be filtered by the Word of God. When I taught my five year old subtraction my goal was not only that he learned the simple mathematic fact of ten minus one equals nine. My goal was much higher. Instead, I took him to Luke 17:12-19 and showed him the story of Jesus healing the ten lepers. He learned that nine went away and one came back giving thanks to Christ and glory to God. When we teach with a biblical mindset, math becomes more than just a lesson. It becomes an exercise in godliness.

My most important goal as a parent is to teach my children to love the Lord God with all their heart, soul, mind and strength, first and foremost! Secondly, would be to love their neighbor as their self. Jesus said that on these two commandments hang all the law and prophets (Matthew 22:36-40). I also want to teach them to work hard (Colossians 3:23), not to impress others with their intelligence or for self-centered achievements, but because in working hard we give God glory. Everything we teach our children can point to God and His glory. While these goals soar above all others and I fail miserably at times, in truth they are the only ones worth pursuing. To see how this is practically applied let us look at a few of the core subjects that most children are taught.

Language

Whether your child is just learning phonics and how to read or he is diagramming sentences and writing papers, you can easily teach with an eternal perspective. What is the goal in teaching my child to read? The most obvious would be that he can read the Bible. The Creator of the universe and of all that is seen and unseen has given His Word in written form so that we can know Him. What better motive for teaching my child to read is there than that? Why should I teach my child how to write, speak, and spell properly? The main reason would be so that he can communicate the glorious gospel to those around him. Remember that one of the goals of discipleship is that the disciple eventually assists in spreading the doctrine of their teacher to others. So we teach them forms of communication so they can communicate to others. Any other achievement should be secondary in importance. Perhaps, in pursuing the English language your child wins a spelling bee or scores high on a test. If so, give God the glory. But do not let those things be your motivation.

The mastering of additional languages can point others to Christ as well. Perhaps your family is learning Spanish for this reason alone. Many hearts have been changed and lives given to Christ in foreign lands. *"And whatsoever ye do in word or deed, do all in the name of the Lord Jesus, giving thanks to God and the Father by him,"* Colossians 3:17. *"Whatsoever ye do"* includes phonics, handwriting, spelling, speech, debate, foreign languages, and language composition.

Math

What does a biblical standard verses a worldly standard look like in teaching mathematics? We have already looked at teaching a small child mathematical operations while using Bible stories, but can we apply this thought to older children? Not too long ago I was reviewing with my son algebraic expressions and equations. This particular lesson covered commutative, associative, and identity properties of addition. Here is what I love about math. It is absolute! If you apply mathematical properties correctly, you will get the correct answer every time without exception. Absolute truths are found everywhere, from the laws of our universe to simple math equations. We accept them, understand them, and live by them. I could have stopped teaching after the math lesson, but I wanted my son to understand a deeper reality. I took the absolute properties of addition and applied the same principle to God's unequivocal truth. God does not change. *"For I am the Lord, I change not,"* Malachi 3:6. Jesus Christ is the same, *"yesterday, and to day, and for ever,"* Hebrews 13:8. And the word of God is absolute. *"Thy word is true from the beginning: and every one of thy righteous judgments endureth for ever,"* Psalm 119:160.

There are many ways in which we can teach our children math using God's principles, but what about our incentives? One very practical motivation we have is so our children will be good financial stewards. My children might not use higher math such as calculus or trigonometry on a daily basis once they become adults, but they will need basic math skills to be able to balance a check book, pay bills, go to the grocery store, or run a business. All of these things, when well done, lend to a good testimony for our Lord. But it could be that our children have a natural gift for mathematics and are able to go on to use their advanced knowledge for the glory of God. Sir Isaac Newton, mathematician and physicist, would be a wonderful example of this very thing.

Science

Biology, ecology, meteorology, geology, and all the other "ologies" are good things to learn. It is good to teach our children about the laws of the universe, but do they know the Maker of the universe? Does my child look at a blade of grass or an animal and see God's handiwork? Have I taught my child to stand back and look at all of creation in awe and wonder? Or am I teaching mere facts in order to pass a test and proceed onto the next course of study? True science will always point us to God. Louis Pasteur, Father of Microbiology, was known to say that the more he studied nature, the more he stood amazed at the work of the Creator. He understood that science brings men nearer to God.

There is a clear difference between teaching science from man's point of view and from God's point of view. One Sunday I was teaching a women's class at my church on creation. I happen to mention the teaching of evolution in our public schools. From the vehement reaction I received from one particular lady, one might have thought I was trying to teach that the earth was flat. She all but called me a liar by insisting that the public schools in Mississippi (where we lived at the time) did not teach evolution. Obviously, since my children did not attend public school, I knew nothing about the subject. Knowing that someone would probably say something, I brought with me the 2010 Mississippi Science Framework that I had downloaded the previous day. I read the following position of the NSTA, which is approved by the Mississippi State Board of Education, word for word to the class.

> "The National Science Teachers Association (NSTA) strongly supports the position that evolution is a major unifying concept in science and should be included in the K–12 science education frameworks and curricula. Furthermore, if evolution is not taught, students will not achieve the level of scientific literacy they need. This position is consistent with that of the National Academies,

the American Association for the Advancement of Science (AAAS), and many other scientific and educational organizations.

NSTA also recognizes that evolution has not been emphasized in science curricula in a manner commensurate to its importance because of official policies, intimidation of science teachers, the general public's misunderstanding of evolutionary theory, and a century of controversy. In addition, teachers are being pressured to introduce creationism, —creation science, and other nonscientific views, which are intended to weaken or eliminate the teaching of evolution."

I pointed out several phrases that were alarming such as, "If evolution is *not* taught, students will not achieve the level of scientific literacy they need" and "teachers are being pressured to introduce creationism, creation science, and other *nonscientific views,* which are intended to weaken or eliminate the teaching of evolution." I lovingly explained that the truth is that teachers are not only expected to teach evolution, but also discredit creation. Any teacher that went against the Board of Education's policy would more than likely face disciplinary actions.

Most Christian parents who teach their children at home are careful in selecting a science curriculum from a biblical point of view. However, we cannot let our guard down. Evolutionist teachings are all around us. The books our children read, the music they listen to, and the television they watch can have subtle evolutionary tendencies.

History

It would be impossible to teach all there is to know about history. There is simply too much information. If we are not careful, this subject can become dull names, tedious dates, and boring facts. However, if we look at history through the sovereignty of God it becomes "His Story". When we realize that a nation will rise and fall by God's hand and that the hearts of kings are stirred by God Almighty, our perspective on history changes. What better opportunity to teach our children biblical morals and values than to have them read about and study godly characters from the past like George Washington? In studying history we can also teach the mistakes from the past so that our children and future generations are not doomed to repeat them. We can learn about important moments in history like when Samuel Morse sent the first telegraph message, *"What hath God wrought,"* taken from the Scriptures. Or perhaps, in our studies of Italy, as we discover the Leaning Tower of Pisa, we can use the opportunity to teach our children spiritual truths about building upon a solid foundation. The possibilities are limitless. Like all of our studies, the study of history can easily guide us to a closer relationship with the God who created history.

Bible

We have previously addressed studying the Bible, but let us not forget that even in studying Scripture we can have a worldly mindset. Every motive should be examined. If we only teach parables from the Bible without practical application, if we only teach the law of God without the grace and love of God, and if we only teach Scripture memorization without meditation, we come dangerously close to creating little Pharisees. It is more important to me that my child loves the Word of God than that my child is able to give a dissertation on the missionary journeys of Paul. While studying the Apostle's life is important, if my child truly loves the Word of God he will enthusiastically learn as much as he can about the Bible. If we develop a love for the Word of God in our children and teach them to diligently seek Him, we give our children a precious gift that can never be taken away.

Learning should be an everyday occurrence and it should not be divided up between secular and spiritual. As a believer, everything should be spiritual. This happens when we incorporate the things of God into our daily studies and academic activities. In doing so it changes not only how we teach, but why we teach. We are no longer just concerned with the outcome, but now with the process and the application. Let's look at an example of teaching my daughter home economics. Perhaps by the world's standard she should learn how to cook, sew, and take care of a baby. But is that enough? In addition to teaching her the fundamentals, by God's standards I would teach her from Titus 2:4-5 to *"be sober, to love their husbands, to love their children, to be discreet, chaste, keepers at home, good, obedient to their own husbands, that the word of God be not blasphemed."* By the world's standards it is good for boys to take a shop or woodworking class. But the application of that would be that my sons learn, *"to study to be quiet, and to do your own business, and to work with your own hands, as we commanded you; That ye may walk honestly toward them that are without, and that ye may have lack of nothing,"* 1Thessalonians 4:11-12. I should teach them not only how to work with their hands, but also in doing that how to become the sole-provider for their families (I Timothy 5:8).

So the questions are: "What are our goals in home education?" And, "By what standards will we choose to live by?" As Christian parents we must keep in mind that we will be accountable for the education of our children not based on the world, but on God and His Word. In that knowledge there is great responsibility, but also great peace. Responsibility in that we will answer to God alone for how we teach and train our children. Peace in that we are not bound by the world's standards for our children.

Practical Application

1. The world's view of success and God's view of success often contradicts one another. We repeatedly see in Scripture godly men and women who were faithful and obedient to Him, but would not be considered successful by the world's standards. Read to your family the 11th chapter of Hebrews and discuss this thought.

2. It is important as parents that we have standards and goals for our children. As Christians, it is even more important that they are made with eternity in mind. Read Colossians 3:1-2 again and as husband and wife, commit to pray about the goals and standards that are made for each of your children.

3. We have talked a lot about having a strong, biblical foundation in our home. Guide your children in a study on the Leaning Tower of Pisa. Use the study as a means to teach your children about building on a solid rock from Matthew 7:24-27.

4. Discipleship is the process by which a disciple (child) is mentored to become more like their teacher (parent). Do you and your spouse live up to the same goals and by the same standards you desire for your children?

5. "Everything we teach our children can point to God and His glory." Make a separate list of subjects taught for each child. Evaluate how each course of study can point your children to their Creator.

Chapter 7
The Practicalities

"Ponder the path of thy feet, and let all thy ways be established."

As we can see, home discipleship involves much more than simply homeschooling our children. However, there is no doubt that the education our children receive plays an important role in the discipleship process. What we put into the minds of our children helps to shape them into who they become. Ultimately, the education of a child will influence the future of the next generation as well. It has been alleged that Abraham Lincoln once said that the philosophy of the classroom of one generation will be the philosophy of the government of the next generation. Whether or not it was Lincoln who voiced this, it is still a true and powerful statement. Remember, discipleship is not just about the here and now. A mark of true discipleship is that the disciple (student) eventually assists in spreading the doctrine (truth) of their teacher (parent) to others. Galatians 6:7 says, *"Be not deceived; God is not mocked: for whatsoever a man soweth, that shall he also reap."* I want the things that I sow into my children to be reaped in their lives and the generation to come. With a world full of choices of things that we can invest into our children, let the Scriptures be preeminent. When we do that, we are sowing seeds of eternal value. These are seeds that will grow into fruit that, with God's blessing, will reproduce for generation after generation.

As Christians, God's Word is the most important thing we can sow into our children, but His Word is not the only thing we need to teach. Our children need to learn math, science, history, language, and more. Therefore, it is vital that we are prayerful in the choosing of our curriculum. I remember, very well, the overwhelmed feeling that came upon me many years ago. As I stood in the midst of a homeschool conference and contemplated homeschooling my four year old, two thoughts whirled through my mind. The first was, "Wow! Look at all these homeschooling families. I won't be alone." The second thought was, "Wow! Look at all this curriculum. How will I ever choose the right one?" Knowledge will play a paramount role in choosing the correct curriculum for your family and the process of learning is never ending. For us, it began many years ago when we started out on our incredible adventure.

Homeschool fairs and conventions are wonderful means to attain information, but they can also be rather intimidating. In fact, for a first time homeschooler, pouring through dozens of catalogs, simply doing an internet search, or just talking with veteran homeschooling families can be daunting. There is a lot of information out there and there are a lot of things to take into consideration.

What foundation is it built on?

There are at least five key factors to consider when choosing a curriculum. The first is to determine what foundation the curriculum is built on. If we are to properly disciple our children, it is imperative that the curriculum we choose has a strong, Biblical foundation. When I look at various curriculums, the subject that needs to be addressed is whether this particular study will give my children a biblical world view. The reason we ask this question is because there is no such thing as amoral education. Everything our children learn will either draw them to God or away from God. We must ask ourselves, as parents, if this is a dynamic worth considering.

Does it fit our family?

We also need to ask if this curriculum fits our family. Just as there are many different types of families, equally there are many different types of curriculums. Some families choose a traditional home education. This is taking the concept of school and bringing it home. Traditional curriculums usually include text books, workbooks, written tests, and core subjects. Others choose to incorporate Unit Studies into their education. I have a friend who is doing a unit study through *Little House on the Prairie* with her three daughters. All three girls, of different ages, will get their math, language, science, history, and Bible in this study. In addition, they learn how to cook and sew throughout the year. Some families choose eclectic, relaxed, or unschooling methods. Still others choose the technique of Charlotte Mason, DVD/video schooling, or internet homeschooling.

We have used various types over the years. I began with the traditional approach, but soon realized that my young son was less apt to sit behind a desk all day. It was more effective to teach him his spelling words while he did jumping jacks, or read to him classic literature curled up on the couch. We found that doing science at the park or in our back yard was successful as well. So we adapted our methods. As we added more children to our family, I found myself doing more unit studies. Now that the children are getting older, we have switched to doing the majority of their schoolwork with a computer program. And, if necessary, chances are we will again alter our approach to fit our family.

When determining what style fits our family we should pay attention to not compare ourselves to other homeschooling families. I have noticed that homeschooling parents seem to be notorious at the comparison game. The Jones children are leaning Latin. The Smith children are three grade levels ahead in math. Our friends at co-op are using the newest science curriculum. And so on. This must be avoided for the well being of the family. The Bible warns us to not compare ourselves with others in spiritual matters. *"For we dare not make ourselves of the number, or compare ourselves with some that commend themselves: but they measuring themselves by themselves, and comparing themselves among themselves, are not wise,"* 2 Corinthians 10:12. The principle applies here as well. It is easy to want to compare ourselves to others, but the lives of others should not set our standards. God's will for our family is the standard we must seek, not God's will for other families. We must seek the Lord and His will for our family and stop comparing ourselves to everyone else. God created each of us in a unique way. He created our family unique. Unless we embrace our differences and seek out God's will for our family, we will constantly struggle in this area.

Is it fun?

Once we have determined the foundation that the curriculum is built upon and whether or not it is God's plan for our family, we should ask ourselves if it is going to be fun. As the old adage goes, "Do what you love and you'll never work a day in your life." Likewise, consider the wisdom behind this: Give a child a love for learning, and he'll never be in school. If we can successfully instill into our children a true love for learning, then the act of studies will not become a chore. This is a concept that I still have to go back to on a weekly basis. Sometimes lessons become mundane, but one of the greatest advantages of home education is that they do not have to be. We have great freedom in how we teach our children. Math facts can be boring, but if you have a daughter who loves to cook you can teach her fractions in the kitchen. She will have so much fun that she will not even realize she is learning. History can be a drab, but if you have an auditory learner you can find some fascinating historical audio dramas to listen to in the car. This will help peak your child's interest in history. Some children struggle with writing, but they are very proficient at sending letters to friends or writing emails. A wise parent will use these avenues to teach their children. My oldest son loves to work with wood; therefore, we have tried to use his passion as an opportunity to teach various subjects of importance.

It must be said, however, that it will be difficult to make everything a child needs to learn fun and exciting for them. My children certainly do not always see the learning process as fun. This does not change the truth behind this principle, nor does it change our goal of instilling a love for learning in our children. One of my children always likes to ask the question, "Why do I need to learn this?" He continues with explaining that it is likely that he will never need this in life. It is then that I take the opportunity to remind him of some important facts. It may be true that unless he becomes an engineer he might not need to know high levels of calculus and trigonometry, but he *will* need to learn how to study. And unless he becomes a history major it is likely that it will not be necessary to memorize all the dates of every war fought; however, he *will* need to be able to sharpen his memorization skills. Studies teach us diligence. And that is unquestionably an attribute worth achieving. All children need to be trained in the art of hard work and that training can come from simply learning higher math or detailed history.

What are others saying?

The Bible speaks a lot about the value of seeking wise counsel. Proverbs 12:15 says, *"The way of a fool is right in his own eyes: but he that hearkeneth unto counsel is wise."* The homeschooling movement has grown over the years. There is a generation of homeschool graduates who are now teaching their own children. Homeschooling groups and co-ops are in abundant. There is easy access to literature and information about homeschooling and curriculums. Homeschoolers do not have to be on an island all by themselves. There is support and connections all around. Parents need to learn to take advantage of all this information. A little research will go a long way in determining if a curriculum is right for your family. Ask around. See what others are saying. Talk to people who have used it. Read the reviews before buying. As one homeschooling mother once told me, "A friendly warning about curricula that doesn't live up to the hype has inoculated me against unnecessary cases of buyer's remorse."

Are we being consistent?

When choosing a curriculum for your children remember these key factors. What foundation is it built on? Does it fit our family? Is it fun? What are others saying about it? And one final thought I would like to offer is on consistency. While consistency does not necessary play a part in which curriculum to choose, it does play a part in whether we become successful in this choice. We have found ourselves having to change a curriculum that was not working during the middle of a school year. But one thing that did not change was the consistency of doing that necessary study. The math curriculum might have changed, but the study of math did not. Perhaps a reading or language curriculum is not working for your family. It is okay to adjust. Just be sure to continue to teach reading and language on some level. Maybe you are unsatisfied with a Bible program, that's okay too. Just be sure your family is reading the Bible every day. A good rule of thumb for younger children is to be consistent in teaching the three R's - Reading, wRiting and aRithmetic.

An essential element in homeschooling is that you, the parent, take the God given responsibility for your child's education. These decisions are important, but you are not left to face them alone. Commit the path of learning your family will take to prayer. Trust in God to lead you. And keep your eyes focused on Him and all the practicalities will work themselves out. *"Let thine eyes look right on, and let thine eyelids look straight before thee. Ponder the path of thy feet, and let all thy ways be established,"* Proverbs 4:25-26.

Practical Application

1. What we put into the minds of our children is a vital part of discipleship. Read Philippians 4:8. What eight things are we told to *"think on"?*

2. Paul said in the following verse, *"Those things, which ye have both learned, and received, and heard, and seen in me, do: and the God of peace shall be with you,"* Philippians 4:9. What is the difference between our children "learning" a truth and "receiving" it?

3. "The philosophy of the classroom of one generation will be the philosophy of the government of the next generation." Do you believe this statement to be true? Have we seen this truth played out in our country?

4. If you have purchased curriculum in the past, what was the most prevalent reason you chose the one you did?

5. Ask yourself these five key factors about your current curriculum. What foundation is it built on? Does it fit our family? Is it fun? What others say? Are we consistent?

Chapter 8
The Individuality

"I will praise thee; for I am fearfully and wonderfully made."

What we put into the mind of our children is an imperative process in discipleship. In the last chapter we addressed the importance of carefully choosing a curriculum for this very reason. One of the items of consideration was whether or not the curriculum was a good fit for our family as a whole. In this chapter we are going to speak to the individuality of each child within the family.

One look at this world we live in and the uniqueness of people who live in it can attest to the creativity of God. Creation displays diversity in such a striking manner. Our world shines with varieties and assortments of plants and animals. Different climates and seasons speak to our Creator's originality. Snowfall testifies to this, for we know that no two snowflakes are exactly the same. And God certainly made mankind with very distinctive characteristics. The Psalmist declares that he is *"fearfully and wonderfully made,"* Psalms 139:14. Man is made in the image of God, yet all look different, act different, behave different, and even learn differently from one another. No two people are exactly the same. If you have multiple children you can attest to this. Children can have the same father and mother, live in the same environment, and be raised in the same manner, yet be completely different from one another.

Uniqueness is a reality, but also a wonderful gift. There is no one else like you and there is no one else like your children. We are all truly one of a kind. God has created each of us special and with a purpose for our life that only we can achieve. As a parent, you have the awesome responsibility to mold and shape your children with their unique strengths and individual character traits. Yet, when it comes to education, society as a whole expects children to be standardized? Why should they all be conformed to the same mold? Why do many have a "one size fits all" attitude with our children? As a homeschooling parent, it is another easy trap to fall into. This is especially true for those of us who were educated in a public system and were constantly conformed to the same standard. But I have learned that it is imperative to adapt to the unique needs, strengths, and weaknesses of each of them. Understanding different learning styles, applying various teaching methods, and helping them develop their unique spiritual gifts can deeply enhance our children's education, the homeschooling experience, and how we disciple each of them.

All three of my children have different learning styles. My oldest son is an auditory learner. He learns best through listening. He is a good reader, but comprehension is at its highest if the text is read out loud. He likes to talk things through and listen to what others have to say. My daughter is a visual learner. She learns best through seeing. Pictures, diagrams, videos, power points, and handouts help to enhance her learning experience. She wants to be shown how to do something other than being told how to do it. My youngest son is a kinesthetic learner. He learns through moving, doing, and touching. He is my hands-on boy who wants to explore the world around him. Do not tell him how to do something and certainly do not do it for him. He learns best by doing it himself. Sitting still for long periods of time is not his strongest feature. Each child has weaknesses to an extent, but they also have strengths we can focus on.

Because each child learns differently, it would be foolish to teach each of them the same way. The greatest Disciple Maker of all taught in various places and ways. Christ did not teach in just one place; He taught in the synagogues, in a ship, sitting on a hillside, in homes, resting at a well, walking on the sea, in the corn field, in cities and villages, on top of a mountain, surrounded by children, riding a donkey, and in the upper room. Christ did not teach in just one manner either. As the Creator of mankind, He would understand man's need for diverse teaching styles. Our Lord stood in the synagogue and read from the book of Isaiah. He taught doctrine and parables for all who would have *"ears to hear"*. Christ also taught using visual illustrations. During His Sermon on the Mount, Christ uses birds and lilies to teach about worry and anxiety. *"Take no thought for your life, what ye shall eat, or what ye shall drink; nor yet for your body, what ye shall put on. Is not the life more than meat, and the body than raiment? Behold the fowls of the air: for they sow not, neither do they reap, nor gather into barns; yet your heavenly Father feedeth them. Are ye not much better than they? Which of you by taking thought can add one cubit unto his stature? And why take ye thought for raiment? Consider the lilies of the field, how they grow; they toil not, neither do they spin: And yet I say unto you, That even Solomon in all his glory was not arrayed like one of these,"* Matthew 6:25-29.

Christ used a penny as an object lesson when tempted by the Pharisees. *"Then went the Pharisees, and took counsel how they might entangle him in his talk. And they sent out unto him their disciples with the Herodians, saying, Master, we know that thou art true, and teachest the way of God in truth, neither carest thou for any man: for thou regardest not the person of men. Tell us therefore, What thinkest thou? Is it lawful to give tribute unto Caesar, or not? But Jesus perceived their wickedness, and said, Why tempt ye me, ye hypocrites? Shew me the tribute money. And they brought unto him a penny. And he saith unto them, Whose is this image and superscription? They say unto him, Caesar's. Then saith he unto them, Render therefore unto Caesar the things which are Caesar's; and unto God the things that are God's. When they had heard these words, they marvelled, and left him, and went their way,"* Matthew 22:15-22.

I have even wondered if perhaps Peter or the other disciples were kinesthetic learners, for Christ often taught them using action and hands on activities. Do you remember the story of Peter walking on water? *"And when the disciples saw him walking on the sea, they were troubled, saying, It is a spirit; and they cried out for fear. But straightway Jesus spake unto them, saying, Be of good cheer; it is I; be not afraid. And Peter answered him and said, Lord, if it be thou, bid me come unto thee on the water. And he said, Come. And when Peter was come down out of the ship, he walked on the water, to go to Jesus. But when he saw the wind boisterous, he was afraid; and beginning to sink, he cried, saying, Lord, save me. And immediately Jesus stretched forth his hand, and caught him, and said unto him, O thou of little faith, wherefore didst thou doubt? And when they were come into the ship, the wind ceased. Then they that were in the ship came and worshipped him, saying, Of a truth thou art the Son of God,"* Matthew 14:26-33. I imagine that Peter learned well the lesson on faith because of the manner in which it was taught. He would never forget the boisterous wind and raging waters. Do you remember the lesson on being a humble servant that Christ taught when He washed His disciple's feet? *"If I then, your Lord and Master, have washed your feet; ye also ought to wash one another's feet. For I have given you an example, that ye should do as I have done to you,"* John 13:14-15. Christ could have told a story about being a humble servant, but showing his disciples impacted them more. Many times the Lord taught using action and hands on activities. After His resurrection, in John chapter 21, Christ taught a powerful lesson on love while cooking a fish dinner.

Having a clear understanding of your child's learning styles can tremendously help with your teaching methodology. For a parent with an auditory learner, finding good quality audio books can be a real treasure. Or, if my son is having a hard time grasping a math concept I have him read it out loud. This always seems to help. I engage him in lots of discussion and have him repeat important concepts back to me. Visual learners can really benefit from instructional DVD's or computer programs. If my daughter is listening to a sermon or a lecture she will often take notes to help absorb all the information. Drawing can also be a powerful teaching tool for visual learners as well. Kinesthetic learners need to be moving. Jumping jacks and spelling words go hand in hand with my kinesthetic learner. I will have my son spell his spelling words over and over again while using up lots of energy. If I am reading history or science I allow him to quietly play with Lego's or let him draw. He absorbs more if his hands are busy. Hands-on science projects are a must for kinesthetic learners.

If you are teaching all of your children the same concept at once, it is important to incorporate all of these learning styles into your teaching. For example, let's say you are expounding on a Bible verse that you want all of them to memorize. You can encourage your audio learner by having the children write a poem to recite out loud or make up a song about the verse. To help your visual learner envision it, encourage them to draw the verse out on a poster board using pictures. Your kinesthetic learner will thrive if you have them act the Bible verse out before the entire family. When implementing these strategies, their learning is being reinforced by their own strengths in a fun and creative way.

Whether you are teaching your children using the traditional method, classical education, unit studies, computer, or online programs consider that one of the greatest benefits to home education is that your children's learning can be tailored to fit their needs. Each child has a different personality. Remembering this will help prevent frustration when that personality clashes with our own. For example, when I am reading or studying I want it very quiet; therefore, naturally I would assume my children should be the same. However, my oldest son - the auditory learner - likes background noise when he's studying. This floors me, but my husband, who is also an auditory learner, says that most assuredly this is helpful. So, I have learned to relax and accommodate my son's learning style. Environment can also play a factor. Some children learn best with it quiet while sitting at a desk. Others can sit at the kitchen table with scores of noise and activity all around them and learn. Still others like to curl up on the couch or learn on a blanket in the backyard.

Not only will our children have different learning styles, but each will have spiritual gifts that need to be discovered. Ephesians 4:7 says, *"But unto every one of us is given grace according to the measure of the gift of Christ."* And I Corinthians 12:7 states, *"the manifestations of the Spirit is given to every man to profit withal."* These gifts are given by our Lord for the strengthening of the body and edification of others. They might include faith, giving, helps, prayers, mercy, music, serving, hospitality, knowledge, wisdom, or writing. In the discipleship process we can encourage our children to discover their unique spiritual gifts and, as they grow in their Christian life, support them in exercising them.

Remember that no one knows your children better than their Creator. We are reminded of this truth by David in Psalm 139:1-3, *"O LORD, thou hast searched me, and known me. Thou knowest my downsitting and mine uprising, thou understandest my thought afar off. Thou compassest my path and my lying down, and art acquainted with all my ways."* When seeking direction in how we teach our children, prayer is certainly one of most valuable assets we have as a parent. Ask the Lord to show you the best way to individually teach your children. He is acquainted with all their ways. He knows everything about them. Trust Him to guide you. Learn to embrace their uniqueness. And be sure to thank God for this blessed opportunity to disciple, teach, mold, and shape these precious gifts.

Practical Application

1. Have you determined what learning styles your children have? Are they auditory learners, visual learners, or kinesthetic learners?

2. Have you determined your learning style? Does your style of learning clash with your children's style of learning?

3. It is important to incorporate each of the different learning styles within your teaching. Teach the following verse to your family this week using all three different learning styles. *"The name of the LORD is a strong tower: the righteous runneth into it, and is safe,"* Proverbs 18:10.

4. God has given each believer a spiritual gift to use for His glory. Read the following scriptures: Romans 12:6-8, 1 Corinthians 12:8-10 and 28-30, Ephesians 4:11, and 1 Peter 4:9-11, and discuss them with your family.

5. There are several spiritual gifts test and surveys online that are free and easy to take. Find one and encourage each family member to discover their God-given gift(s).

Chapter 9
The Opposition

"Marvel not, my brethren, if the world hate you."

Jesus said in John 15:18-19, *"If the world hate you, ye know that it hated me before it hated you. If ye were of the world, the world would love his own: but because ye are not of the world, but I have chosen you out of the world, therefore the world hateth you."* As Christians, we are called a *"peculiar people"* (Titus 2:14, I Peter 2:9). At one time we walked *"according to the course of this world"* (Ephesians 2:2), but not anymore. As children of God, we are *"children of light"* (I Thessalonians 5:5). Where we once walked in the flesh, we now walk in the spirit (Romans 8:1).

Therefore, we are different, strange, and odd. And that's just for starters. Add to the equation a choice to educate and disciple your children at home and expect to meet resistance from those in the world. At some point, we should expect that our lifestyles will offend people.

Take a journey back in time to a few generations ago in America. How easy would it be to offend a person thirty, forty, or fifty years ago? The older generation voices of an era when the majority of people would not only be offended to hear a crude word spoken, but would not even tolerate it. Not too many years ago people would be offended to see open sin paraded around in public. At one time people would be offended to see children speaking disrespectfully to an elder. Our country and flag was greatly honored and to show disrespect to either was offensive. And the thought of someone openly condemning Christianity in America was unthinkable. The generations of the past were easily offended by insulting behaviors, filthy language, open immortality, anti-patriotism, and a blatant disregard for spiritual matters.

But, oh, how the times have changed! It seems as though the deliberate decay of our culture is not only tolerated, but joyfully embraced. The pendulum has swung, and now the offenses which must not be tolerated are of a different caliber. Today the offenses come in the form of Christianity, absolute truth, holy living, the name of Jesus Christ, submission to authority, and of course, the Christian homeschool movement.

I remember the first time I realized that there were people

who were offended by our family's lifestyle. It was the summer after our first year of homeschooling. The friend who had introduced our family to home education was sitting next to me in a ladies Bible study class. We were discussing the benefits and joys of the year. I had commented that I was so thankful the Lord opened our eyes to our responsibility as parents to educate our children. During the discussion, others joined in asking questions. After the class was over a lady approached me who had been very offended that we had so openly discussed homeschooling as a valid option for Christian parents. She had been a public school teacher for twenty years and in her own words, "had never seen anything taught to the detriment of Christians in public school." She was adamant in that public schools were safe and unmistakably the best option for all Christians. Although I was new to homeschooling and could not clearly articulate my position, it had not been that long ago that I was in public schools myself. I distinctively remember all the evil that I was exposed to at an early age from teachers and peers alike, not to mention the anti-God philosophy that was so often taught.

    While it was the first time that I have viewed such opposition to home education, it certainly was not the last. There was once a lady in our church who showed apparent disdain toward our family. I remember asking my husband one day after services what I could have possibly done to her. "She obviously does not like me," I said. "I've gone out of the way to be kind and friendly to her and her family." My husband, who knew how hard I had been trying said, "Sweetheart, it is nothing you have done. Our lifestyle is offensive."

Over the years we have come to realize that the choices we have made regarding our family is contrary to many people even in the church. We know the church should be a safe place filled with encouragement and love. The world should be absent from the church, but unfortunately there are times when it seeps in and influences the church body. This was one of those times. Not everyone who claims Christ believes as we do. My husband and I believe that Scripture teaches a very distinct way of living as a child of God. As a woman, I believe that part of my high calling is to be a help meet to my husband (Genesis 2:18), to live in subjection to him (I Peter 3:5), and to be a keeper at home (Titus 2:5). We believe that the husband, as the head of the family, will be responsible to God for the education and upbringing of the children (Ephesians 6:4, Proverbs 4:1-7). He is to oversee all their learning about God and His world. And daily, he is to teach God's Word to his family (Deuteronomy 6:5-9). As his help meet, I play a major role in the daily teaching of our children. At the heart of all we do lies biblical truth. And because biblical truth is being taught less and less, we really should not be surprised when people are offended.

While we somewhat expect this opposition from the world, it is disheartening when it comes from other Christians. One could argue that there are those who simply claim the title yet bear no fruit of righteousness. Many times it is these people who are antagonistic to those trying to live their life according to the Bible. But I also must say that is not always the case. Many Christians simply have never been taught the truth. For several generations, our society has believed that families should pursue the "American dream" at all cost. In this pursuit, the foundation of the biblical family has been cracked. Sadly, many churches have lacked in biblical teaching necessary to rebuild the family. So now, when a family pushes against the flow of society, by holding to their convictions from the Word of God, they often experience a backlash. Perhaps, you have experienced such criticism from family, friends, church members, or even pastors. It seems that a few months cannot pass without hearing a testimony from a family to this extent. They are homeschooling because of biblical conviction and due to the amount of criticism they receive one would think that they have purposely set out to destroy the lives of their children.

Maybe you have experienced the same criticism. You hear comments like, "You shelter your children too much." Let me say something to that. Dear friend, do not let the world dictate to you lies from the enemy. It is a good thing to shelter your children. God shelters us and I am so glad He does! When the storms of life come, His children run into His arms of safety. *"The name of the LORD is a strong tower: the righteous runneth into it, and is safe,"* Proverbs 18:10.

Then there are those who want to remind you that, "Your children will rebel!" As far as children rebelling, perhaps they will.

But I know that children will often do exactly what they are trained to do. Some parents believe the lie that at a certain age all children will come to rebel against the teaching of their parents. When a parent believes this and expects his child to rebel the parent will not be disappointed. They should be realistic enough to know that children might, but it is foolish to expect it of them. My husband and I will bring our children up in the way they should go and hold on to the promise that they will not depart from that training (Proverbs 22:6).

Another common criticism voiced is, "Your children will not know how to deal with the 'real' world!" People assert this notion without a clear understanding of our goals. The objective in Christian homeschooling and discipleship is not teaching our children how to "deal with the real world." I do not want to teach my children how to merely survive this life. As believers in Christ we are called to be overcomers! *"For whatsoever is born of God overcometh the world: and this is the victory that overcometh the world, even our faith,"* 1 John 5:4. As children of God, not only do we overcome this world, but we overcome the wicked one (I John 2:13-14). We overcome his servants (I John 4:4). We overcome sin and death (I Corinthians 15:54-57). And we overcome evil (Romans 12:21). This is what we desire to teach our children. We do not want them simply "dealing" with the "real" world. We want them to overcome it!

Do not be discouraged when you face opposition. Do not be surprised by the world's criticism. As you probably have learned by now, one does not have to be on the front lines of the homeschool movement to be attacked. You do not have to be publicly declaring the truths found in Scripture from every mountain top to offend the world. All you have to do is live your life quietly and simply in holiness. Raising your family according to God's standards is enough to have the world hate you. Your very lifestyle is condemning to those around you.

Consider the story of Noah. *"By faith Noah, being warned of God of things not seen as yet, moved with fear, prepared an ark to the saving of his house; by the which he condemned the world, and became heir of the righteousness which is by faith,"* Hebrews 11:7. I have heard this story my whole life. I have been taught that Noah, being a preacher of righteousness (2 Peter 2:5), preached to the world the coming judgment of God. In my mind I always assumed that it was his preaching that condemned the world. But this passage in Hebrews does not tell us that the world was condemned by his preaching. It was his life that condemned the world. Noah moved with fear and prepared an ark to save his family. It was his faith, fear, and obedience to God that condemned the wicked.

Now, move forward a few thousand years. Consider a faithful father called of God to lead his family. He reads in the Bible of the coming judgment. He sees the warnings from his Heavenly Father. He is moved with fear and works hard to build an ark of safety for his family. He rejects this world and does that which is necessary to save his house. He toils and labors to lead his wife and disciple his children in the ways of the Lord. And in doing it all, he condemns the world around him.

But unlike Noah, who knew only his family would be saved (Genesis 6:17-18), we are not alone. There are many other families who are striving to follow the Lord. There are many fathers who take their God-given responsibility seriously and seek to save their homes from worldly destruction. There are many mothers who are coming along side and fulfilling their God-given role. There are many children who are being brought up in the nurture and admonition of the Lord. There are families who still stand strong. Do not give up. Do not be discouraged. Know that your work will not be in vain! The day of rejoicing is fast approaching! *"That ye may be blameless and harmless, the sons of God, without rebuke, in the midst of a crooked and perverse nation, among whom ye shine as lights in the world; Holding forth the word of life; that I may rejoice in the day of Christ, that I have not run in vain, neither laboured in vain,"* Philippians 2:15-16.

Practical Application

1. Have you experienced criticism and opposition from the world regarding your choice to homeschool your children? Have you experienced opposition in your church or from other Christians?

2. Considering the current state of public education, why do you think so many Christian people are still adamant that public education is the best choice?

3. Look up the following verses in Revelation about *"he that overcometh."* Revelation 2:7, Revelation 2:11, Revelation 2:17, Revelation 2:26, Revelation 3:5, Revelation 3:12, Revelation 3:21, Revelation 21:7.

4. Do a study this week on the life of Noah from Genesis chapter 6 – chapter 9.

5. You should not be alone in this journey. Have you found a good local church that supports your decision to homeschool and encourages you as a parent to be responsible in the discipleship of your children?

Chapter 10
The Results

"And he shall be like a tree planted by the rivers of water."

Everywhere you turn you can find a television ad, brochure, or spokesperson addressing the need to save the earth and plant a tree. Society is constantly being indoctrinated to believe in "Mother Earth" and "Global Warming". There are organizations, websites, and even a nationally celebrated observance dedicated to tree planting and care. As believers and children of God, unequivocally we are to be good stewards of God's creation. God gave man the responsibility to have dominion over this earth and to *"dress it and to keep it,"* Genesis 2:15.

Unfortunately, the passion many have for our planet is often misplaced. You see, there is great irony when man worships creation and disregards the Creator. Romans 1:25 explains that man, *"changed the truth of God into a lie, and worshipped and served the creature more than the Creator."* With all of that said, I will give the tree loving faction credit in one area. They are investing in the future. People who plant trees rarely enjoy the full benefits of the shade that the tree will bring. They do, however, recognize the fact that someone else in the future will. There is wisdom in looking toward the future and planning ahead. An old Chinese Proverb says, "If you think in seasons, plant cereals; if you think in decades, plant trees; if you think in centuries, educate your children."

As a parent, I have to ask myself if I am properly investing in the future. Am I thinking about the centuries to come? Do my husband and I have a multi-generational vision? Is our family concerned with embracing God's truth and passing it on to our children and our children's children? Are we thinking about our family's godly heritage three and four generations from now? Are we planting spiritual trees by the rivers of water that will bring forth much fruit? Are we watering these trees with living water and daily cultivating them with the Words of Life? Are we carefully caring for each tree as the Master Gardener would have us to? To answer these questions in an absolute affirmative is my heart's desire.

There is wisdom and knowledge, that God gives in His

Word, to accomplish this very task. If you are seeking, a great place to start is Psalm One. In this Psalm the writer gives us a striking antithetical parallelism. The Hebrew poet shows us the contrast between the blessed man and the ungodly man.

> *"Blessed is the man that walketh not in the counsel of the ungodly, nor standeth in the way of sinners, nor sitteth in the seat of the scornful. But his delight is in the law of the LORD; and in his law doth he meditate day and night. And he shall be like a tree planted by the rivers of water, that bringeth forth his fruit in his season; his leaf also shall not wither; and whatsoever he doeth shall prosper. The ungodly are not so: but are like the chaff which the wind driveth away. Therefore the ungodly shall not stand in the judgment, nor sinners in the congregation of the righteous. For the LORD knoweth the way of the righteous: but the way of the ungodly shall perish."* Psalm 1:1-6

This Psalm visibly teaches antithetical principles. As Christian parents we should purpose to teach this model to our children as well. God's Word is full of contrasting opposites. *"For the wages of sin is death; but the gift of God is eternal life"* Romans 6:23. *"Hatred stirreth up strifes: but love covereth all sins"* Proverbs 10:12. *"Depart from evil, and do good"* Psalm 37:27. All through Scripture opposites are clearly revealed: life and death, love and hate, good and evil, saved and unsaved, narrow way and broad way, blessed and cursed, wise and foolish, fruitful and withered, etc. When we teach our children balanced views, they understand consequences of both good and bad in life. We do not want their life to be *"like the chaff which the wind driveth away"* as the Psalmist states, but *"like a tree planted by the rivers of water."*

Notice that the blessed man *"walketh not in the counsel"*, takes advice, or learns from the ungodly. Nor does the blessed man *"standeth in the way of"* or abides with sinners. Nor does he *"sitteth in the seat of the scornful"*. He does not continually dwell with those who scoff or mock. This precept should be applied to all areas of our children's life. And it certainly includes all forms of education our children receive. Homeschooling families are usually very careful to guard who teaches their children, whether it is the mother, father, older siblings, another Christian in a co-op class, or teachers at church. However, we must be watchful; for humanistic, secular, and ungodly philosophy can still creep in unaware. This can happen through books read, media watched and listened to, or even through outside relationships our children have. Therefore, we must strive to be ever diligent, constantly on guard, and ever pursuing the best for our children.

With God's mercy and grace the result of discipleship is what every Christian parent prays for. *"His delight is in the law of the Lord."* The vision my husband and I have for our family and the main goal in discipleship is to teach our children to love God and delight in His Holy Word. Everything else our children learn is secondary. As stated before, in teaching our children how to read, the primary goal is to learn to read the Bible. In teaching them language skills, the main objective is for them to be able to communicate the glorious gospel to those around them. In teaching them science and math principles, the purpose is to point them to God, His truth, and His marvelous creation. In teaching them history, we want them to learn from godly men and women and the mistakes people have made so that they will not repeat them. In teaching our children life skills, the objective is to prepare them to be good examples to the lost world, good stewards of God's blessings, and light in this dark world. We desire to give our boys a good education, not to fulfill selfish desires they might have, but so that they can be prepared to provide for their families. By being good providers they will be giving God glory through their work. We desire to give our daughter a good education, not so that she can chase after selfish dreams. Instead, a good education will help her pursue God's perfect plan for her life.

My husband often reminds me that these principles cannot be taught alone. They must be taught, but then embraced as truth and lived out in our own lives. Remember, more is caught than taught. I can "teach" my children biblical principles every day, but if they do not see their mother living by those same principles then I am teaching something I never intend to teach. Our children must see their parents delighting in the law of the Lord. They need to see us meditating upon Scripture. They need to see us growing in our walk and deeply rooted in the Truth. Why? Because we know that a child of God deeply rooted can weather all the storms of life.

Our family moved south, close to the gulf coast, a year after Hurricane Katrina stormed onto shore. As we drove across the coastline, the most noticeable thing to us was the trees. Very few survived. Some were completely destroyed. Roots and all were ripped up. But a small number of strong trees did survived. They, nevertheless, were not left untouched. They were twisted and bent by the fierce winds. But even the warped shape of these trees served as a precious reminder that their roots were deeper and stronger than the hurricane. This can also serve as a reminder to us. When the enemy sends the winds of trials and troubles into our homes we can survive by digging deep into the rich soil that is watered by the rivers of Truth.

Children who are taught this life principle and see their parents living out the truth will themselves learn to love God and delight in His law. Children who delight in the law of the Lord will meditate upon it day and night. Children who meditate upon Scripture will naturally begin to grow in grace and knowledge. And children that grow in grace and knowledge will become fruitful. This is a precept that we, as Christian parents, can trust in; *"whatsoever he doeth shall prosper."* That is the result of tree planting and the desire of every parent who wishes to disciple their children in the ways of the Lord.

Practical Application

1. Do you agree with the old Chinese Proverb that states, "If you think in seasons, plant cereals, if you think in decades, plant trees, if you think in centuries, educate your children"?

2. Read Romans 1:18-32. Make a list of the character traits that we see in those *"who changed the truth of God into a lie, and worshipped and served the creature more than the Creator."*

3. Does your family have a multi-generational vision? If you do, write it down so you will have it for years to come.

4. We know that the blessed man, *"walketh not in the counsel of the ungodly, nor standeth in the way of sinners, nor sitteth in the seat of the scornful."* Give modern examples of what this walking, standing, and sitting might look like in our own lives. List ways of how the husband, wife, and children can avoid this.

5. Commit to memorize Psalm 1 together as a family.

Chapter 11
The Distinction

"A man of understanding is of an excellent spirit."

The calling of discipleship is a high calling. The goals, standards, and pursuits for the Christian family listed throughout this book are indeed high. God's standards for all Christians are high. There is no doubt that it will take diligent work to accomplish all God has called us to do. Many will never try feeling the vision is too lofty. Many will try only to give up. What will make our experience different from others?

In the book of Daniel, we are told a story of a young man of noble descent. This young man, whom the book is named after, faced great trials throughout his life. Daniel's story begins:

> *"In the third year of the reign of Jehoiakim king of Judah came Nebuchadnezzar king of Babylon unto Jerusalem, and besieged it. And the Lord gave Jehoiakim king of Judah into his hand, with part of the vessels of the house of God: which he carried into the land of Shinar to the house of his god; and he brought the vessels into the treasure house of his god. And the king spake unto Ashpenaz the master of his eunuchs, that he should bring certain of the children of Israel, and of the king's seed, and of the princes; Children in whom was no blemish, but well favoured, and skilful in all wisdom, and cunning in knowledge, and understanding science, and such as had ability in them to stand in the king's palace, and whom they might teach the learning and the tongue of the Chaldeans. And the king appointed them a daily provision of the king's meat, and of the wine which he drank: so nourishing them three years, that at the end thereof they might stand before the king."* Daniel 1:1-5

Nebuchadnezzar had ordered that a number of children of *"the king's seed, and of the princes"* be transported to Babylon where they would serve him in an official capacity. Now imagine the young Jewish man, Daniel, being torn away from his family and placed in a pagan land filled with great temptations. His parents were no longer there to impart wisdom. He stood accountable to

God alone. Those who know the story will remember all the tests Daniel faced throughout his life. In the first chapter of Daniel we see where Daniel and his friends were tested in what foods he would eat. *"But Daniel purposed in his heart that he would not defile himself with the portion of the king's meat, nor with the wine which he drank: therefore he requested of the prince of the eunuchs that he might not defile himself,"* Daniel 1:8. After ten days of eating vegetables and drinking water, Daniel and his friends were healthier than those that ate of the king's meat. When they later stood before the king, he was quite impressed. *"And in all matters of wisdom and understanding, that the king enquired of them, he found them ten times better than all the magicians and astrologers that were in all his realm,"* Daniel 1:20.

In the second chapter of Daniel we see him faced with yet another test. Nebuchadnezzar had a troubling dream that he could not remember. He ordered his wise men to reveal his dream and its interpretation. When they could not do as he commanded, the king *"was angry and very furious and commanded to destroy all the wise men of Babylon,"* Daniel 2:12. God gave Daniel the dream and interpretation and Daniel stood again before King Nebuchadnezzar. *"The king answered unto Daniel, and said, Of a truth it is, that your God is a God of gods, and a Lord of kings, and a revealer of secrets, seeing thou couldest reveal this secret. Then the king made Daniel a great man, and gave him many great gifts, and made him ruler over the whole province of Babylon, and chief of the governors over all the wise men of Babylon,"* Daniel 2:47-

48. Again, Daniel had proven to be a very impressive young man.

Sometime later a different king, King Belshazzar, hosts a banquet and sees a hand appear out of nowhere write a message on his wall. Again the king's wise men could not read the writing or make known the interpretation. The queen tells the king about Daniel and he is brought to stand before Belshazzar. *"I have even heard of thee, that the spirit of the gods is in thee, and that light and understanding and excellent wisdom is found in thee,"* Daniel 5:14. Daniel interprets the writing on the wall and predicts God's coming judgment upon Belshazzar. That night Daniel's prophesy came true when Darius the Median took the kingdom and slew Belshazzar. Daniel was then promoted by Darius. *"Then this Daniel was preferred above the presidents and princes, because an excellent spirit was in him; and the king thought to set him over the whole realm,"* Daniel 6:3.

Throughout his life Daniel faced a lion's den, continued to interpret dreams, and received divine visions and revelation from God. In it all, there was one consistent thing in his life. He was filled with wisdom and had an *"excellent spirit"*. Proverbs 17:27 says, *"A man of understanding is of an excellent spirit."* Everything Daniel faced, he faced with excellence. We can learn a lot from him, for he was a man of distinction.

In dealing with the discipleship of our children, we should endeavor to carry it out it with excellence. Striving for excellence will be what distinguishes successful discipleship from poor or even nonexistent discipleship. My husband preaches to his congregation about the importance of excellence in our lives. Every action, objective, and form of ministry should be done with excellence. The reason is simple, yet profound. We carry on this way because of the Almighty God we serve and who we are in Him. Daniels wisdom and excellent spirit was a testimony to God and His glory. As a child of God, this thought should permeate not only ministry, but every aspect of life. Whether it is our marriage, parenting, the discipleship of our children, or our work; we should be intentional in doing it with excellence.

When we fail to strive for excellence, it can become dangerously easy to go through life accomplishing tasks in a mediocre fashion. I have seen this in my life. It is not because I want to, but simply because of the busyness of life. Discipleship is time consuming, (as are many things in life such as ministry, homeschooling, parenting, and striving to have a strong marriage). In fact, I will just say it right now. There is not enough time in the day. There are too many things that I want to teach my children. There are too many curriculums that I want to try. There are too many character traits to instill and Bible verses to memorize. There are too many outside activities that I want them to participate in. There are too many ministries of good value. Add that to the fact that all of my children need to be taught with different styles and on different levels. Then there is a house to run that comes with a vast amount of time-consuming responsibility. Then we have external influences that pull on our lives and take up time like family, friends, sports, hobbies, and recreation.

But please do not misunderstand; the life of a Christian should be full of activity, as should the life of a Christian family. We are to be productive and that leaves no place in our life for laziness. But when you add it all up, sometimes this plethora of activity develops into mediocrity. Trying to do too much will cause us to do none of it well. We can go through life doing numerous good things, but this can lead to the family being spread too thin. When this happens, our attention becomes divided, the family looses focus, priorities are misplaced, and nothing is done with excellence. In his corporate book, *Good to Great*, Jim Collins says that "Good is the enemy of great." He goes on to say, "Few people attain great lives, in large part because it is just so easy to settle for a good life." While he is referring to the business world, the statement is just as true for the Christian family. We do a lot of good things in life, but it is often at the expense of missing out on the greatest.

How does this apply to our home and life in general; and just what does it have to do with discipleship? If we are to conquer mediocrity in life and strive to disciple our children to the best of our ability, we must learn to live the simple life. To do this, we need to be intentional in the choices we make. Several years ago my son made a statement that I will never forget. It had been an exhausting week filled with activity. We were constantly on the go and gone most evenings. So I had determined this particular day would be different. Throughout the day I was intentional and focused. Gone was the attitude of quickly finishing our schoolwork so we could move on to other things. It was replaced with an attitude of joyfully teaching my children and giving them a love for learning. We were relaxed and the house was peaceful. While the children enjoyed lunch, I did a few extra chores making sure the house was in order. Then I put dinner in the Crockpot so when Dad came home our evening meal would be prepared. That afternoon, as a gentle rain fell, I sat down in the living room with my computer and a cup of hot tea. Soft music flowed from the kitchen as my two younger children played a game together. My oldest son was sitting on the couch reading a book and said, "Mom, I love days like today. Life is calm and peaceful." That simple statement spoke volumes to me. Simplicity makes life joyful. Simplicity creates room for reflection and growth. Simplicity allows peace to flood your soul. This is why the Psalmist reminds us to, *"seek peace, and pursue it."* Psalm 34:14b. The opposite of peace is chaos and disorder, and we all know that being too busy leads to both.

    In order to live a simple life we must learn to say "No!" We cannot do it all. Let me correct that statement. It is not an issue of whether we can do it all or not. The issue is that we should not even try. What are the most important things in your life? Are you able to focus on those with excellence? I have to ask myself this question often. The truth is that I like saying "yes". However, wisdom is often exuded more when we say "no" than when we say yes to every single thing. Steve Jobs understood this concept and it was his resolute attitude that solidified his successful results in life. At an Apple Worldwide Developers Conference in 1997 he said, "People think focus means saying yes to the thing you've got to focus on. But that's not what it means at all. It means saying no to the hundred other good ideas that there are. You have to pick carefully. I'm actually as proud of the things we haven't done as the things I have done. Innovation is saying no to 1,000 things." Did you catch that? He was more proud of the things he did not do than the things he did. Would adopting this line of thinking revolutionize a typical homeschool day? Would it bring about transformational changes in the way we disciple our children?

I like the way that Karen Andreola encourages young ladies to strive for excellence in her book *Beautiful Girlhood.* In it she says, "No girl can rise higher than her ideals. It is impossible to attain higher things than we strive for; and few even reach their ideals. So it is imperative that a girl set before her good and pure ideals, that she set her mark high. It is better to aim at the impossible than to be content with the inferior." Does the idea of being content with the inferior alarm you? Most of us do not want that for ourselves or our children. We want to aim high and teach our children to do the same. We want it to be said that the spirit of God is in us and *"that light and understanding and excellent wisdom is found"* in our family.

As believers, we understand that we are to strive with excellence toward the highest goal. Paul stated, *"I press toward the mark for the prize of the high calling of God in Christ Jesus."* Philippians 3:14. Just what is the prize of the high calling? It is to be like the perfect Son of God. Impossible you say! The goal is too lofty. Many will wonder why we should even bother trying, but we try because of what God has done in our lives. We try because of our testimony to the world. We try because the very name in which we call ourselves means to be Christ-like. We strive to live *"soberly, righteously, and godly, in this present world,"* Titus 2:12. We strive to have the same mind of Christ (Philippians 2:5) and to walk in Him (Colossians 2:6). Holiness is our standard (1 Peter 1:16). *"Not as though I had already attained, either were already perfect: but I follow after,"* Philippians 3:12.

Even though to live as the perfect Son of God is unattainable this side of heaven, we grasp that one day we will reach our goal. We are promised that the day will come when we will be like Christ. *"We know that, when he shall appear, we shall be like him; for we shall see him as he is."* 1 John 3:2. Until that glorious day, with the power of the Holy Spirit working in our lives, we keep striving for excellence in all we do. It is this that distinguishes us from all others.

Practical Application

1. Daniel faced many troubles and trials during his life, yet he came through them victoriously. Have troubles and trials left you and your family feeling defeated? What can we learn from Daniel about overcoming the trials of life?

2. Daniel *"purposed in his heart that he would not defile himself."* What does it mean to purpose in your heart? Will it take a purposing in our hearts to be able to successfully disciple our children?

3. Being too busy can greatly hinder the discipleship process. Families that are too busy simply do not have the time to invest in proper discipleship activities. Evaluate your schedules. Is busyness in your family a problem that needs to be addressed?

4. In his corporate book, *Good to Great*, Jim Collins says that "Good is the enemy of great." Considering this thought, have good things in your life robbed you of the greatest?

5. I John 3:2 states that one day, when Christ will appear, we *will* be like him. The following verse explains that every person that *"hath this hope in him purifieth himself, even as he is pure,"* 1 John 3:3. What does this mean to you?

Chapter 12
The Conclusion

"Let us hear the conclusion of the whole matter: Fear God, and keep his commandments."

We live in a fast and furious society. Everything is microwave quick. We know it is true. If we have to wait more than sixty seconds in a drive-thru window we get impatient. If we have to stand in line at the bank for more than five minutes we become restless. For those who do not believe me, I challenge you to wait a few minutes after the stop light turns green and see how long it takes for people to start honking. Patience is a virtue long gone in our society. Everyone wants immediate results. From weight loss, to learning a new trade, to having a new kid by Friday, we expect things to happen instantaneously. But discipleship does not happen right away. It cannot be rushed. It will not be hurried. In addition, a disciple cannot be mass-produced. Each disciple has to be taught, molded, and shaped individually. And that will take time. We need to remember that the perfect disciple maker spent three years, day in and day out, developing His disciples. Should we expect to do less?

We must never forget that our children belong to God and He has entrusted the discipleship of them to us. What an awesome responsibility! The teaching process begins at birth. We are teaching our children from the moment those sweet babies are born. We teach them the sound of our voice. We teach them to sit up. We teach them to walk. We teach them to talk. We teach them that the stove is hot and outlets are dangerous. We teach them about love; we teach them right from wrong; we teach them about God and the world around us. Then we move on to knowledge, wisdom, and academics.

As much as we teach our children and as much as we desire them to learn, the truth is that we will never teach them enough. Solomon understood this. He wrote an entire book on discipleship and throughout it he taught his son with diligence. In the book of Proverbs, Solomon tells his son to hear his instruction, receive his words, forget not his law, attend to his words, attend to his wisdom, and keep his commandments. Then in Proverbs 23:26 Solomon says, *"My son, give me thine heart, and let thine eyes observe my ways."* In all of our teaching, sometimes we forget that it is the child's heart we are after. Discipleship is about developing a relationship. It can be done no other way.

It has been said many times already that no one has a more vested interest in your children than you do. But perhaps I should rephrase that statement. The truth is that God does have a more vested interest in your children than even you do. As much as we want our children to come to Christ and live holy, God-pleasing lives, our Lord desires it even more. We cannot produce godly children. Only God can do that.

- God desires them to be saved.

"For this is good and acceptable in the sight of God our Saviour; Who will have all men to be saved, and to come unto the knowledge of the truth," 1 Timothy 2:3-4.

"The Lord is not slack concerning his promise, as some men count slackness; but is longsuffering to us-ward, not willing that any should perish, but that all should come to repentance," 2 Peter 3:9.

- God does the drawing.

"No man can come to me, except the Father which hath sent me draw him: and I will raise him up at the last day," John 6:44.

"And I, if I be lifted up from the earth, will draw all men unto me," John 12:32.

- God will do the work of salvation in their hearts through repentance and faith.

"For by grace are ye saved through faith; and that not of yourselves: it is the gift of God: Not of works, lest any man should boast," Ephesians 2:8-9.

"Testifying both to the Jews, and also to the Greeks, repentance toward God, and faith toward our Lord Jesus Christ," Act 20:21.

- And it is God that sanctifies and enables them to live godly lives.

"But we are bound to give thanks alway to God for you, brethren beloved of the Lord, because God hath from the beginning chosen you to salvation through sanctification of the Spirit and belief of the truth," 2 Thessalonians 2:13.

"For the grace of God that bringeth salvation hath appeared to all men, Teaching us that, denying ungodliness and worldly lusts, we should live soberly, righteously, and godly, in this present world," Titus 2:11-12.

We simply cannot force our children to become godly and it would be to their detriment to even try. Our job as Christian parents is to make sure our children have godly parents. Did you catch that? For emphasis, let me repeat it. It is not our job to produce godly children; it is our job to make sure our children have godly parents and trust that God will do the work in their lives.

While it might seem contrary, if we want to properly disciple our children we need to focus first on our own lives. An attempt to disciple them in the ways of the Lord without living out true faith ourselves is futile and hypocritical. With that being understood, when our lives are pleasing to God, we will be influential to our children. We will be determined to live like Christ lived. Jesus was a disciple maker; therefore, we will be disciple makers as well. And because no one (but God) has a more vested interest in your children than you, the discipleship of them should be our number one priority.

Discipleship is a real sacrifice; it is more than giving them an education and it is more than teaching good morals. The discipleship process is pouring our lives into another person. The reason is multifaceted. It is because we love them and want the very best for their lives. It is also for the reason that our Lord commands us. And it is because through discipleship we change the world. The world needs changing, wouldn't you agree? Christ taught the twelve so that they would teach others. This is our goal. I am investing in my children truths and principles that one day I desire to be taught to my grandchildren and great-grandchildren.

When we strive to obey the commands of Christ, we change the world one person at a time and we are filled with joy knowing that we have obediently followed in the footsteps of the Great Disciple-Maker himself.

Much more could be said about the discipleship process. But in truth, enough has already been said. You see, many of us do not need more knowledge on the topic. Many times, we are already educated well beyond our level of obedience. It is not more information we need on the subject, but more wisdom to apply what we already know. This wisdom can only come from God and His Word. Seek Him out. Study His Word. Be encouraged toward obedience and see the need to disciple your children in His ways, knowing that the world will be changed one person at a time.

Let us end with the same words Solomon ended with as he discipled his son. *"And further, by these, my son, be admonished: of making many books there is no end; and much study is a weariness of the flesh. Let us hear the conclusion of the whole matter: Fear God, and keep his commandments: for this is the whole duty of man. For God shall bring every work into judgment, with every secret thing, whether it be good, or whether it be evil,"* Ecclesiastes 12:12-14.

Practical Application

1. The discipleship process will take years. Are you committed to investing your life to disciple your children?

2. Do you believe that God has the best interest of your children at heart? Does this encourage you to spend more time in prayer to for them?

3. The last verse in the Old Testament ends with a warning. Look up Malachi 4:6. What will happen if the hearts of fathers are not turned to their children and the hearts of the children are not turned to their fathers?

4. The conclusion of the whole matter has two sides. The first is that we are to *"fear God"*. Look up the following passages on the fear of the Lord: Deuteronomy 6:2, Joshua 4:24, I Samuel 12:24, 2 Kings 17:39, Psalms 2:11, Psalms 111:10, Psalms 147:11, Proverbs 9:10, Matthew 10:28, 1 Peter 2:17.

5. The second is that we *"keep his commandments."* Look up the following passages about the commandments of the Lord: Exodus 20:6, Deuteronomy 8:6, I Kings 8:61, Psalms 112:1, Psalms 119:47, Proverbs 10:8, John 14:15, John 15:10, I John 2:3-4.

"Discipleship is a real sacrifice; it is more than giving children an education and it is more than teaching good morals. The discipleship process is pouring our lives into another person."

Our Favorite Resources

Non-Fiction Books:

How to Bring your Children to Christ...& Keep Them There: Avoiding the Tragedy of False Conversion, Ray Comfort and Kirk Cameron

Family Driven Faith: Doing What it Takes to Raise Sons and Daughters, Voddie Baucham Jr.

The Truth War, John MacArthur

The Quest for Character, John MacArthur

Family Man, Family Leader, Philip Lancaster

Family Fiction:

The Peleg Chronicles Series, *www.matthewchristianharding.com*

Lamplighter Collection Books, *www.lamplighter.net*

Family Resources:

Hearts of the Fathers Family Discipleship Resources, *www.heartsofthefathersresources.com*

Practical Tips on Raising the King's Kids, Dr. Travis Plumlee, *www.travisplumlee.com*

Evangelism Resources:

The Way of the Master, Ray Comfort, *www.wayofthemaster.com*

Homeschool Magazine:

Home School Enrichment, *www.homeschoolenrichment.com*

Curriculum Reviews:

Home Educating Family Reviews, *www.hedua.com/reviews/*

About The Author

Kimberly Williams is a pastor's wife, homeschooling mother, author, and most importantly a disciple of Jesus Christ. Living in NW Arkansas with her husband and three precious children, her career is her family. With the loving support and encouragement from her husband and the amazing grace of God, Home Discipleship has not just become a title of a book, but a way of life. Each year brings new experiences, creates wonderful memories, and brings her family closer together.

Kimberly has contributed to various homeschooling magazines and websites. Her passion for writing has one purpose, to point others to Jesus Christ. She is the author of <u>Living Out the Word</u>, a series of expository ladies Bible studies. In addition to writing, Kimberly has a heart for speaking to women and encouraging them in their daily walk with the Lord. She points them to God's Word and challenges them to be a true help meet to their husbands and loving mothers to their children. She uses practical application, storytelling, laughter, and most importantly, the Word of God. Visit: *http://livingouttheword.net/speaking-schedule/* for a list of speaking topics.

In her spare time, Kimberly loves to read, play the piano, write songs and poetry, chat on Facebook, and blog at *www.untilthedaydawn.wordpress.com*. She would love to hear from you at *www.homediscipleship.net*.

www.ingramcontent.com/pod-product-compliance
Lightning Source LLC
Chambersburg PA
CBHW061447040426
42450CB00007B/1250